The
Complete
Freshwater Fishes
of the British Isles

First published 1979
by A & C Black (Publishers) Ltd.
35 Bedford Row, London WC1R 4JH
ISBN 0 7136 1937 6
© 1979 Jonathan Newdick

Newdick, Jonathan
    The complete freshwater fishes of the
British Isles.
    1. Fishes, Fresh-water – Great Britain
I. Title
597'.0920'41   QL633.G7

ISBN 0-7136-1937-6

Printed in Great Britain by
W. S. Cowell Ltd, Ipswich

The Complete Freshwater Fishes of the British Isles

Jonathan Newdick

Adam & Charles Black · London

CONTENTS

INTRODUCTION

This book contains illustrations of mature specimens of all those fishes which are likely to be found in fresh and brackish water in the British Isles. There are fifty four species which fall into this category, some of which exhibit widely differing forms due either to the effects of their environment or as a result of selective breeding, and some of which live partly in the sea. Some recently introduced fish which do not have established breeding colonies are illustrated only with line drawings while wholly marine species which occur exceptionally in brackish water are excluded, although a few which are similar to fresh water species are mentioned as an aid to identification. The descriptions apply to mature fish although immature fish are described where these are quite different from the adults. Where sexual differences are not described it can be assumed that the sexes are similar. Finally, those hybrids which are on record as having bred under natural conditions are also included.

The plates

All the plates are reproduced the same size as the original paintings and most contain a silhouette of the Minnow, *Phoxinus phoxinus* which is drawn to the same scale as the fish depicted. This gives an approximate but immediate indication of the size of the fish and for this purpose it can be assumed that the Minnow is 10cm long. The fish on those plates where the Minnow is omitted are depicted life size. Plants and animals which are included on the plates are not necessarily to scale.

Distribution maps

The maps are intended only as an approximate guide to the distribution of each species but they are based on recent evidence and within the constraints of the scale adopted they present a fairly reliable indication of the range of each fish described.

Text diagrams

The diagrams used throughout the text are intended primarily as aids to identification and are not drawn to any particular scale.

GLOSSARY

One of the aims of this book has been to try and keep the text simple and no attempt is made to describe the internal organs and functions of fish with the exception of the mention of gill rakers, vomer and pharyngeal bones where these are helpful aids to identification. However, the major external organs and features which are useful taxonomic characters are used in the descriptions of species, and this has necessitated the following explanation of terms.

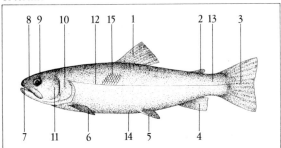

1-6. Fins. Except for the adipose fin these consist of rays either hard (often spiny) or soft, which are joined by thin membranes. The number of rays is often significant in identification. In the texts the word *deep* is used to describe the distance between the body and the outer edge of the fin, while the word *long* is used to describe the distance between the first and last rays. **1.** Dorsal fin. Where there is more than one dorsal fin that nearest the head is known as the first, the next one the second and so on. **2.** Adipose fin. A fleshy posterior dorsal fin without rays which is found in the salmon family and a few other families.
3. Caudal fin. **4.** Anal fin. **5.** Pelvic fins (paired).
6. Pectoral fins (paired).
7. Mouth
8. Nostril
9. Iris
10. Operculum
11. Pre-operculum
12. Lateral line. Sensory canal running along the length of most fish connected to the scales by pores and therefore usually visible. The number of scales along the lateral line is often of taxonomic importance.
13. Caudal peduncle
14. Keel
15. Scales (not present on all species)
Gill rakers. Comb-like structures situated beneath the operculum which prevent water-borne particles passing into the delicate respiratory organs. These are particularly important in identifying the shads.
Pharyngeal bones. Strong bones in the back of the mouth of some species which are adapted for crushing food. These are particularly important in identifying members of the carp family.

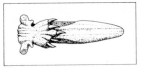

Typical salmonid vomer
(Char, *Salvelinus alpinus*)

Vomer. Toothed bone in the roof of the mouth of some species which is an important factor in the identification of certain members of the salmon family.
Barbels. Tactile sensory organs on some species which take the form of long (sometimes very long) fleshy growths and which are usually situated around the mouth.
Tubercles. Small fleshy growths which are usually associated with spawning.
Redd. Hollow in the gravel bed of a stream in which certain members of the salmon family shed their eggs.

Larva. The developmental stage of most fish between hatching from the egg and absorbtion of the yolk sac.

Typical larva (Bream, *Abramis brama*)

Yolk sac. The yolk of the egg which remains attached to the larva after hatching and which is gradually digested by the larva before it begins to feed conventionally.
Parr. Immature stage of certain members of the salmon family especially Salmon, *Salmo salar* and Trout, *S. trutta*.
Parr marks. Large approximately oval dark patches along the sides of parr.
Anadromous. Spawning in fresh water but maturing in the sea.
Catadromous. Spawning in the sea but maturing in fresh water.

Mouth positions

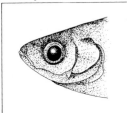

Superior (Bleak, *Alburnus alburnus*)

Terminal (Roach, *Rutilus rutilus*)

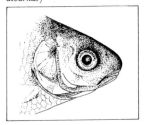

Inferior (Silver bream, *Blicca bjoerkna*)

Strictly speaking the Petromyzonidae or lampreys are not true fishes although they are generally accepted as being so. They are scaleless, completely boneless and their body structure is formed of cartilage. They do not possess jaws and instead the mouth is modified to form a sucking disc with which they parasitise fishes and other animals. The breeding cycle is complex, there being a larval stage which may last up to six years and there are three British species, two of which are anadromous.

1 River lamprey

Lampetra fluviatilis, Linnaeus 1758

Distribution

The River lamprey is an indigenous species which is widespread and generally common although it is scarce in northern Scotland.

Habitat

The River lamprey spends some time in the sea although it probably does not swim far from the shore. In fresh water it is found in estuaries, rivers and streams and also lakes which are easily accessible from the sea. They are catholic in their choice of water but prefer a stream with a sandy or stony bed for the spawning site.

Spawning

Usually in the autumn but sometimes in the spring the anadromous River lamprey leaves the sea and makes for the spawning streams. During spawning physiological changes occur, the most noticeable being the growth of an anal fin on the females. Colourless eggs measuring 1mm in diameter are laid in the spring among gravel, after which the adults die. The larvae live buried in mud for five or six years after which they metamorphose at about 12cm long and migrate to the sea where they remain for one to two years.

Size

The normal adult length is between 30 and 40cm although a length of 50cm is not uncommon.

Diet

While buried in mud the larvae consume tiny organisms and bacteria. The adults prey on various coastal and estuarine fishes by attaching themselves to their hosts and sucking the blood which does not coagulate due to a secretion produced by the lamprey.

Identification and similar species

The River lamprey is a uniform greyish cream colour. It has no mouth in the true sense, this being replaced by a sucking disc. There is no operculum but instead there are seven small circular gill openings on each side.

Eel, Anguilla anguilla

The resemblance of the River lamprey to the Eel is superficial and it can be distinguished by its absence of paired fins and by its mouth.

Sea lamprey, Petromyzon marinus

If the River lamprey cannot be separated from the Sea lamprey by its colour and smaller size then the best means of identification is by examination of the mouth structure.

Brook lamprey, L. planeri

The River lamprey has two distinct dorsal fins whereas the Brook lamprey has one which has a conspicuous dip towards the front.

Larvae

The larvae of all three lampreys are difficult to identify. The River lamprey larva can be distinguished from the Sea lamprey larva by the fact that the former has no pigment apparent in the skin below the gill openings. The Sea lamprey larva does have pigment here. However, the differences between the larvae of the River lamprey and Brook lamprey are not so well defined as this and the two can only be reliably identified by detailed examination.

No hybrids involving the River lamprey have been recorded from British waters.

See also plates 2, 3 and 42.

Mouth structure

---

1 River lamprey, *Lampetra fluviatilis*.
Also illustrated: River lamprey larva; Hazel, *Corylus avellana*; Fennel leaved pondweed, *Potamogeton pectinatus*.

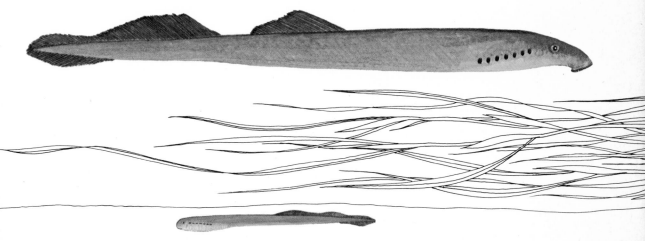

2 Sea lamprey

Petromyzon marinus, Linnaeus 1758

Distribution

Mouth structure

While the Sea lamprey is indigenous to Britain and is found around almost all the coastline and in most rivers which have easy access to the sea, it is more frequent in England and Wales than in Scotland and Ireland.

Habitat

The Sea lamprey spends most of its life in fresh water as a larva where it lives buried in the mud downstream of the spawning area. Mature fish live in the sea until ready to spawn when they may be found in clean streams and rivers which have beds of gravel or stones.

Spawning

The Sea lamprey is anadromous and during May and June a large depression is made in the bed of a clean flowing stream in which the female lays clear eggs measuring 1.2mm in diameter. Often a male will mate with more than one female and directly after spawning the adults die. The eggs hatch in one to two weeks and the larvae are blind and toothless, spending between five and six years buried in mud until maturity when they make their way to the sea. On entering the sea they measure about 20cm long and they remain there for one to three years, growing quickly to reach a length of about 70cm when ready to spawn.

Size

The length of mature adults is between 60 and 90cm although most specimens are not more than 75cm long.

Diet

In the larval stage the Sea lamprey feeds exclusively on tiny organisms and detritus which it finds in the soft mud. The mature specimen is parasitic on a wide variety of marine fishes and also crustaceans to which it attaches itself by means of its powerful sucking disc and from which it drains the blood after wearing away the skin with its toothed tongue.

Identification and similar species

The back and sides of the Sea lamprey are yellowish brown to grey mottled with black, and the belly is white or grey. There are two distinct dorsal fins and behind each eye are seven gill openings.

Eel, Anguilla anguilla
The mouth and the lack of paired fins and operculum readily distinguish the Sea lamprey from the Eel.
River lamprey, Lampetra fluviatilis
The River lamprey is generally smaller than the Sea lamprey and its body is not mottled. Out of the water the best means of identification is by examination of the mouth structure.

Brook lamprey, L. planeri
The Brook lamprey is very much smaller than the Sea lamprey and it has a single dorsal fin.
Larvae
The larva of the Sea lamprey is coloured both above and below the gill openings whereas both the River lamprey and the Brook lamprey lack pigmentation below the gill openings.

No hybrids involving the Sea lamprey have been recorded from British waters.
See also plates 1, 3 and 42.

---

2 Sea lamprey, *Petromyzon marinus*.
Also illustrated: Sea lamprey larva; Stonewort, *Chara aspera*.

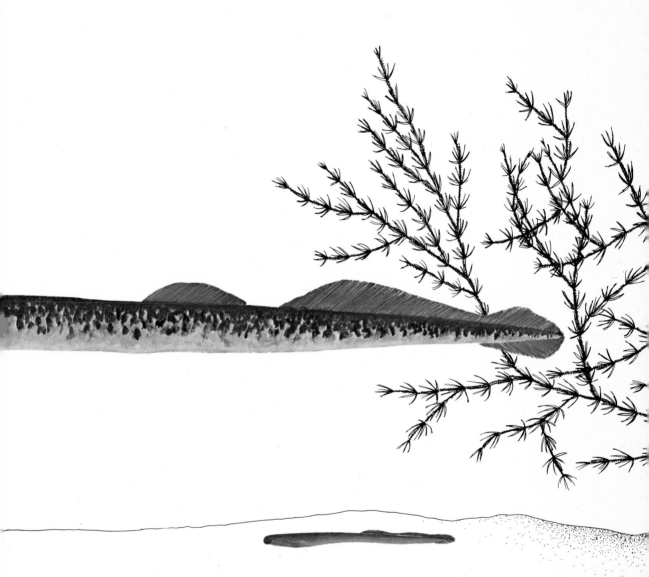

3 Brook lamprey

Lampetra planeri, Bloch 1784

Distribution

This indigenous species is probably the most common of the three lampreys occuring in Britain. It is frequent in all parts of the region except the north of Scotland.

Habitat

The Brook lamprey is non-migratory and spends its whole life in rivers and streams with sandy or gravelly beds.

Spawning

Clear eggs measuring just under 1mm in diameter are laid in depressions among stones in clean flowing water between April and June, after which the adults die. The eggs hatch in a little under a week and live downstream of the spawning grounds in mud or among rotting leaves where the water flow is minimal. They begin meta-morphosis in the autumn five or six years after hatching and the process is complete by the following spring when they prepare to spawn.

Size

This, the smallest of the British lampreys, can grow to 25cm in length but is normally not more than 20cm.

Diet

The larvae feed on a variety of tiny organisms and detritus but the adults do not feed at all although they have a small sucking disc with weakly developed teeth.

Identification and similar species

The back and sides are greyish brown, the belly is yellowish, there is one dorsal fin and seven gill openings behind each eye.

Eel, Anguilla anguilla

The resemblance of the Brook lamprey to the Eel is superficial and it can be distinguished by its lack of paired fins, its mouth and its gill openings.

River lamprey, L. fluviatilis and Sea lamprey, Petromyzon marinus

Both these species which are much larger than the Brook lamprey have two distinctly separate dorsal fins.

Larvae

The larva of the Brook lamprey can be distinguished from that of the Sea lamprey by virtue of the fact that it has no pigmentation below the gill openings, whereas that of the Sea lamprey does. However, the larvae of the River lamprey and Brook lamprey are more difficult to tell apart and can only be reliably separated by detailed examination.

No hybrids involving the Brook lamprey have been recorded from British waters.

See also plates 1, 2 and 42.

Mouth structure

---

3 Brook lamprey, *Lampetra planeri*.
Also illustrated: Brook lamprey larva; Water crowfoot, *Ranunculus fluitans*.

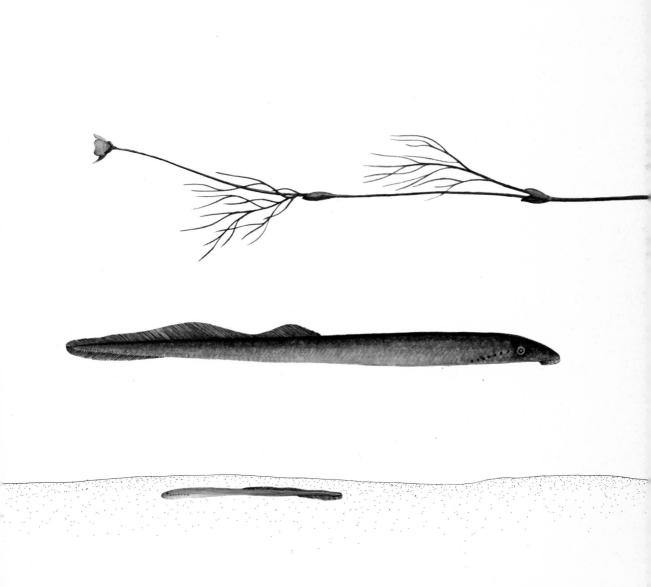

The Acipenseridae or sturgeons are a primitive group of large fishes which are characterised by having longitudinal rows of bony plates along the body and no scales. They are commercially valuable for the roe of the female which is sold as caviar, and for their flesh, but due to the combined effects of over-fishing and pollution of their spawning rivers they are becoming increasingly uncommon. Only one species is found in British waters.

4 Sturgeon

Acipenser sturio, Linnaeus 1758

Distribution

The indigenous Sturgeon is a rare visitor to British waters. It can be expected to occur in almost any estuary and may swim some distance up larger rivers.

Habitat
Most of the Sturgeon's life is spent in the sea and it only enters rivers to spawn, or as is the case in Britain as an occasional vagrant.

Spawning
The Sturgeon is anadromous and ascends rivers to the spawning grounds in spring and early summer where grey eggs measuring 2.5mm in diameter are laid. After spawning the adults return to the sea and are followed two or three years later by the young fish which mature in about eight years. However, the Sturgeon has never been known to spawn in British waters.

Size
The Sturgeon is one of the biggest fishes occurring in British waters, where it may grow to 350cm although the usual length is between 150 and 250cm. At one time even larger specimens were known (up to 500cm) but with the increasing rarity of the species these bigger fish are now almost unknown.

Diet
The Sturgeon uses its sensitive barbels to locate food and its long snout to stir up soft mud. The small creatures that are disturbed are then sucked up by the mouth which can be protruded to form a short tube.

Identification
The Sturgeon has a dark grey back, greyish sides and a pale grey or white belly. There are five rows of bony plates along the body, one on the back, one on each side and two along the belly. The snout is long with two pairs of barbels midway between its tip and the mouth and the upper lobe of the caudal fin is much longer than the lower lobe.

There are no similar species and no hybrids involving the Sturgeon have been recorded from British waters.

4 Sturgeon, *Acipenser sturio*.
Also illustrated: Black headed gull, *Larus ridibundus*.

At one time the shads, which are the only British fresh water representatives of this family, were a valuable food source. However, a combination of over-fishing and pollution of their spawning grounds has brought their exploitation on a commercial basis practically to an end. The two species occurring in British rivers are both fairly uncommon anadromous fish which probably do not swim far from the shore. They tend to form large shoals even at spawning time and both have a single dorsal fin, no lateral line and thick transparent membranes across the front and rear of the eyes.

5 Allis shad

Alosa alosa, Linnaeus 1758

Distribution

The Allis shad is an indigenous estuarine species which occurs on the west coast of England, especially in the Severn estuary. It is also present in western Ireland, western Scotland and to a lesser extent in some south coast estuaries. It was once found and may still occur in the Firth of Forth.

Habitat

The Allis shad lives mainly in estuaries and coastal waters and in the spawning season it swims far up rivers but as a rule does not enter streams. It is not able to negotiate waterfalls and man-made obstacles.

Spawning

The adults swim up rivers during April and May and spawning takes place in May and June when large clear eggs measuring 4.5mm in diameter are shed in flowing water. After spawning, the adults return to the sea and the eggs which fall to the bottom hatch in about a week. The larvae are 10 to 12 mm long. Growth is rapid at first and they descend to the sea when they are between one and two years old and measure between 10 and 18cm.

Size

The length of the mature Allis shad is between 25 and 45cm although it may grow to 60 or 70cm.

Diet

The diet consists almost exclusively of small organisms especially water fleas, shrimps and other crustaceans.

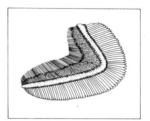

Gill rakers

Identification and similar species

The Allis shad is relatively deep bodied especially towards the head. The back is bluish green, the sides silvery green, the belly is white and the fins are small and pale grey except for the caudal fin which is darker. There are 70 to 80 lateral scales.

Twaite shad, A. fallax

The two shads are very similar although the Allis shad is a rather bigger species and while it may have one or two black spots on the body to the rear of the operculum it never has a row of black spots. The Twaite shad usually does have such a row on each side. The main difference is in the number of gill rakers in the first gill arch. The Allis shad has more than 60 whereas the Twaite shad always has less than 60 and usually about 40.

No hybrids involving the Allis shad have been recorded from British waters.

See also plate 6.

5 Allis shad, *Alosa alosa*.
Also illustrated: Canada geese, *Branta canadensis*.

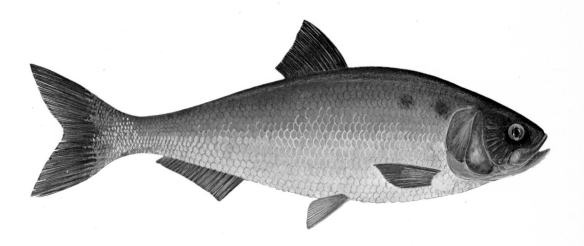

6 Twaite shad

Alosa fallax, Lacépède 1803

Distribution

The indigenous Twaite shad is more common than the Allis shad, *A. alosa*, being found around most of the coastline of Britain. It tends to be more frequent on western coasts and is most common in south west Ireland.

Habitat

Like the Allis shad this species is anadromous but it does not swim far upstream and is found mainly in estuaries and tidal reaches of rivers.

Spawning

In May and June large clear eggs measuring 4.5mm in diameter are deposited on the river bed where they remain for about five days until they hatch. The larvae immediately begin a gradual downstream movement and grow quite quickly, reaching from 12 to 14cm after a year and mature when between three and five years old.

Size

Generally smaller than the Allis shad, the Twaite shad averages from 30 to 40cm in length but some specimens reach 50cm or more.

Diet

The food of the Twaite shad consists mainly of invertebrates but in addition young fish including Eel, *Anguilla anguilla* and Herring, *Clupea harengus* are eaten.

Identification and similar species

The back is bright bluish green, the sides and belly silvery with a greenish sheen and the sides of the head are often golden or yellow. The keel is serrated between the throat and the front of the anal fin and there is a row of 6 to 8 dark spots between the head and the rear of the dorsal fin. There are 60 to 70 lateral scales.

Many races of the Twaite shad, some of which are regarded as subspecies, have been recorded from the mainland of Europe and one landlocked subspecies known locally as the Goureen is found in lakes in Killarney. It grows to a maximum length of 25cm and spawns in shallow areas of the lakes.

Allis shad, A. alosa
For the differences between the two shads see under Allis shad, page 14

No hybrids involving the Twaite shad have been recorded from British waters.
See also plate 5.

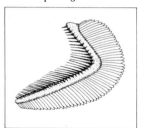

Gill rakers

---

6 Twaite shad, *Alosa fallax*.
Also illustrated: Common mussel, *Mytilus edulis*.

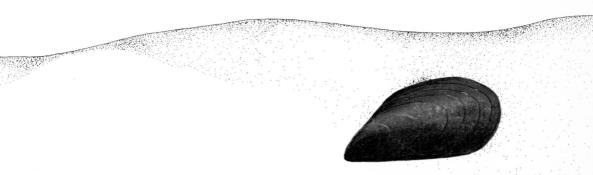

The majority of the Salmonidae, or salmon family, live either entirely in cool fresh water or are anadromous. Six species are found in British waters and all have an adipose fin and a small pointed flap above the pelvic fin base, and being carnivorous all have well developed jaws. Many species, especially the Trout, *Salmo trutta* and Char, *Salvelinus alpinus* have evolved different forms to suit their particular local conditions and at one time some of these forms were considered to be distinct species. Today however, most authorities regard them as geographical races.

7 Salmon

Salmo salar, Linnaeus 1758

Distribution

The indigenous Salmon has decreased in numbers in the past hundred years and although it is still doing so it is a common fish, being found throughout the British Isles although it is scarce in the south east of England.

Habitat

The Salmon spends much of its life in the sea either inshore or as far away as Greenland, and enters rivers to spawn. The rivers chosen are clear and clean and although usually fast flowing are not necessarily so. It is also found in some lakes.

Spawning

Spawning takes place between October and January in running water when large orange eggs measuring 6mm in diameter are shed in redds among gravel. After spawning the females immediately return to the sea but the males may remain to mate with other females after which they too drift downstream. At this stage they are very susceptible to disease and many die but those which reach the sea recover quickly to return to the spawning grounds (not necessarily the same rivers) eighteen months later. Occasionally a third spawning is made and very rarely a fourth. The eggs remain in the redds for some time and most hatch between April and May when the larvae measure about 20mm in length. They live off their yolk sacs until they begin to feed conventionally about six weeks later and although maturity is reached between two and four years they may not migrate to the sea until their fifth year.

Size

Growth is slow in fresh water and Salmon rarely measure more than 25cm long when they migrate to the sea, but thereafter they grow quickly. The length of adults may be anywhere between 40 and 90cm and some grow to 120cm.

Diet

Young Salmon eat invertebrates of all types while bigger specimens take a wide variety of fish and crustaceans.

Identification and similar species

In the sea both sexes have a bluish green back, silvery sides spotted with black and a white belly. In fresh water the male has a greenish brown back, the sides are brownish or pink with black spots edged with pink or orange, the fins are dark bluish grey or brown and the lower jaw is often hooked. The female lacks the pink tint and the hooked jaw and there are 120 to 130 scales along the lateral line. Salmon parr are bluish grey with 10 to 13 parr marks usually with red spots between them. The dorsal fin may be slightly spotted and contains 10 to 12 rays, the adipose fin is grey and there are less than 3 spots on the operculum. (See page 22.)

Trout, S. trutta

The Salmon and Sea trout are very similar and the differences are given under Trout, page 20.

No hybrids involving the Salmon have been recorded from British waters. See also plates 8 and 9.

Two Pacific salmon apart from the Humpback salmon, *Oncorhynchus gorbuscha*, page 26, may be present in British waters. The Chum salmon, *O. keta* is established in the White Sea and may occur in almost any estuary while the Coho salmon, *O. kisutch* has spread from French rivers to the Channel Islands and may be found in southern England. The Chum salmon has 150 to 160 scales along the lateral line and the Coho salmon has 120 to 150, and more than 12 rays in the anal fin: the indigenous Salmon has less than 11 rays in the anal fin.

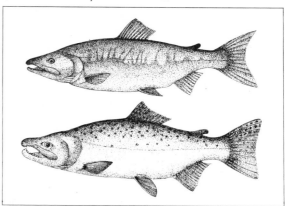

Chum salmon, *Oncorhynchus keta* (top), and Coho salmon, *O. kisutch*, both breeding males.

7 Salmon, *Salmo salar*.
Also illustrated: Cormorant, *Phalacrocorax carbo*.

Trout

The Trout is an exceptionally variable species both in habit and in form and colour. At the beginning of this century many 'species' were recognised but today most authorities group all these together and regard the Trout as a single species whose variations are due mainly to environmental factors. Nevertheless, it is usual to separate the anadromous form (usually called Sea trout) from the non-migratory form (Brown trout) and these two types are described here.

8 Sea trout

Salmo trutta, Linnaeus 1758

Distribution

The Sea trout is indigenous, being found around almost all of the coast of Britain and often far inland but it is less frequent in the Midlands and the south east of England.

Habitat
Most unpolluted clear, cool streams with access to the sea provide suitable conditions for the Sea trout.

Spawning
Mature Sea trout ascend rivers either in spring and summer or in autumn, and spawning takes place from October to January when orange eggs measuring 4mm in diameter are deposited among gravel in running water. The young remain in fresh water for up to three years and the descent to the sea usually takes place in the spring. The mature fish return to the spawning rivers between two and five years after entering the sea when they measure 25 to 50cm in length.

Size
The normal adult length is between 25 and 60cm although they do grow to 90cm.

Diet
The Sea trout consumes large numbers of invertebrates. Bigger specimens also take fish and crustaceans.

Identification and similar species
The body of the Sea trout is usually a silvery bluish green colour with a darker back and white belly. The back and sides are sparsely spotted with dark blue or black and there are also spots on the dorsal and caudal fins and on the operculum. The colour and intensity of the spots of the males increases during the spawning season and they develop a hooked lower jaw. There are 120 to 130 scales along the lateral line.

Salmon, S. salar
The Sea trout is often almost indistinguishable from the Salmon but the Salmon has a thinner caudal peduncle and the rear edge of its caudal fin is usually more or less forked whereas that of the Sea trout is usually fairly straight. The upper jaw bone of the Sea trout extends to, and often beyond the rear of the eye: that of the Salmon rarely reaches as far as this. The Sea trout has 13 to 16 scales between the adipose fin and the lateral line whereas the Salmon has 10 to 13, but the most decisive difference between the two species is in the construction of the vomer. The front of that of the Salmon is toothless but that of the Sea trout does contain teeth.

No hybrids involving the Sea trout have been recorded from British waters.
See also plates 7 and 9.

---

8 Sea trout, *Salmo trutta*.
Also illustrated: Kingfisher, *Alcedo atthis*.

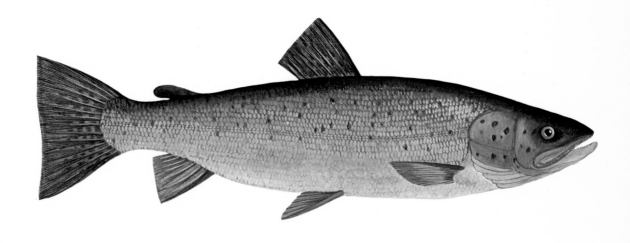

9 Brown trout

Salmo trutta, Linnaeus 1758

Distribution

A very common species, the Brown trout is found in almost all of the British Isles.

Habitat

Most rivers, streams and lakes which are clean, reasonably high in oxygen and which have access to suitable spawning grounds are likely to contain populations of Brown trout.

Spawning

The Brown trout breeds from October to January when large orange eggs measuring 4mm in diameter are shed in redds among gravel in running water. The eggs hatch after several weeks when the larvae measure about 20mm in length. They live off their yolk sacs for a month or so and drift downstream a little way before they begin feeding. Growth is variable, depending on the locality, and maturity is reached between two and three years when they measure from 15 to 20cm in length.

Size

The length of the non-migratory form of the Trout is governed by its surroundings and adults may measure from 20 to 50cm in length.

Diet

The Brown trout consumes large numbers of invertebrates. Bigger specimens also take fish and crustaceans.

Identification and similar species

In colour this is an extremely variable species although the shape remains constant. Generally it is brownish or greenish with a darker back and paler belly, but greyish blue specimens are common and some fish are so dark as to be practically black. There are many black spots on the head and body and also some red spots which are usually circled with blue. The lower jaw is long, reaching past the rear edge of the eye and in old males it is often hooked. There are 120 to 130 scales along the lateral line.

Trout parr have 9 or 10 parr marks on each side, the dorsal fin is spotted with black and contains from 8 to 10 rays, the adipose fin is usually orange and there are almost always more than 3 black spots on the operculum.

Char, Salvelinus alpinus and Brook char, S. fontinalis

Both Chars have smaller scales than the Brown trout,

there being 180 to 240 along the lateral lines of both species.

Rainbow trout, S. gairdneri

The differences between Brown trout and Rainbow trout are listed under Rainbow trout, page 24

Hybrids

The Brown trout occasionally hybridises with the Brook char and the offspring are similar to both parents in shape but are marked with bars rather than spots.

See also plates 8, 10, 11, 12 and 56.

Salmon parr

Trout parr

9 Brown trout, *Salmo trutta*.
Also illustrated: Bullhead, *Cottus gobio*; **Fennel** leaved **pondweed**, *Potamogeton pectinatus*.

10 Rainbow trout

Salmo gairdneri, Richardson 1836

Distribution

Wild colonies only

The Rainbow trout, a native of the north western United States and western Canada, has been introduced widely to British waters. It is most common in England but Wales, Ireland and Scotland all have substantial populations. Most of these however are constantly being reinforced by artificially bred fish and if it were not for this the Rainbow trout would be a rare species, there being very few entirely wild populations in Britain.

Habitat

This trout is most often introduced into lakes but it also occurs in clear rivers and streams.

Spawning

Where spawning occurs naturally it takes place between October and March when large orange eggs measuring 4mm in diameter are shed in reeds among gravel in running water. Rainbow trout grow quickly and mature after two or three years.

Size

The adult length varies between 25 and 45cm while the maximum is in the region of 70cm.

Diet

The adult Rainbow trout is primarily a fish eater although this diet is supplemented by invertebrates. The food of smaller specimens consists almost entirely of invertebrates.

Identification and similar species

The Rainbow trout is variable in colour but it usually has a dark greyish blue back and a pale greyish blue belly. It always has a reddish or purple band running from the jaw to the caudal fin and is more or less covered in black spots, these being absent only from the belly. The dorsal, adipose and caudal fins are also heavily spotted and there are 120 to 150 scales along the lateral line.

Brown trout, S. trutta

While the Brown trout is one of the most variable of fresh water fishes it never has a prominent band of colour along the sides as the Rainbow trout does. In addition its spots may be red or orange but those of the Rainbow trout are black only.

Char, Salvelinus alpinus

The Char has smaller scales than the Rainbow trout, there being 180 to 240 along the lateral line.

No hybrids involving the Rainbow trout have been recorded from British waters.

See also plates 9 and 12.

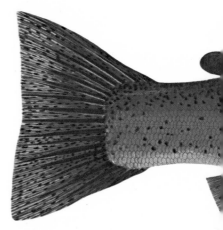

10 Rainbow trout, *Salmo gairdneri*.
Also illustrated: Downy emerald dragonfly, *Cordulia aenea*.

11 Humpback salmon

Oncorhynchus gorbuscha, Walbaum 1792

Distribution

The Humpback salmon was introduced from the northern Pacific Ocean to the Barents Sea in the 1950s and has been recorded a few times as an occasional vagrant in coastal waters of Scotland and northern England.

Habitat

The Humpback salmon spends almost all of its life in the sea and only enters fresh water to spawn. It prefers clear rivers and streams and tends not to swim far upstream.

Spawning

Large orange eggs measuring 5mm in diameter are deposited among gravel in running water during September and October after which the adults die. The larvae have a large yolk sac from which they obtain most of their nourishment until they swim downstream to the sea in the spring. However, the Humpback salmon has never been recorded as having bred in British waters.

Size

This Pacific salmon is usually smaller than the indigenous salmon, the average adult length being 40 to 60cm.

Diet

Like the indigenous salmon the food of the Humpback salmon consists of invertebrates and fish.

Identification

The Humpback salmon has a deep body with a blackish green back and silver sides and belly. The brown dorsal and caudal fins are spotted with black and the lower fins are pale greyish green or white. During the spawning season the males have pink sides more or less blotched with brown, the body becomes very deep and the jaws are hooked, (see page 28). There are 180 to 220 tiny scales along the lateral line.

There are no similar species and no hybrids involving the Humpback salmon have been recorded from British waters.

11 Brook char

Salvelinus fontinalis, Mitchill 1815

Distribution

The Brook char was introduced from North America at the beginning of this century and although widely distributed it is rare.

Habitat

This char is best suited to cool rivers and streams particularly those among mountains but it is also found in cool clear lakes.

Spawning

The Brook char breeds throughout the winter months at any time from October to March, when orange eggs measuring 3.5mm in diameter are laid among gravel in either flowing or still water. Maturity is reached between two and four years later.

Size

The usual adult length is between 25 and 35cm although in favourable conditions the Brook char can grow to a length of 45cm.

Diet

Young Brook char feed almost exclusively on invertebrates while bigger specimens also take small fish.

Identification and similar species

The colouration is variable but usually the back is deep olive mottled with paler spots and bars, the sides are brownish green or pink with yellow and red spots and the belly is pink or white. There are 180 to 240 tiny scales along the lateral line.

Char, S. alpinus
For the differences between Char and Brook char see under Char, page 28.

Brown trout, Salmo trutta
The Brown trout has 120 to 130 lateral scales.

Hybrids
The Brook char hybridises with the Brown trout and the offspring are similar to both parents but are marked with bars rather than spots.

See also plates 9, 12 and 56.

11 Brook char, *Salvelinus fontinalis* (top), and Humpback salmon, *Oncorhynchus gorbuscha* (bottom).
Also illustrated: Water moss, *Fontinalis antipyretica*.

12 Char

Salvelinus alpinus, Linnaeus 1758

The Char is an extremely variable species and throughout its wide range, which extends from North America through Europe to northern Asia, numerous subspecies have been described, some of which are anadromous. Those occurring in British waters are non-migratory and are regarded as forms of the subspecies *S. a. willughbii*. They are much smaller than the anadromous types and about fifteen varieties have been described.

Distribution

The indigenous Char is widely distributed throughout Scotland and Ireland, occurs locally in Wales but is absent from England apart from the Lake District.

Habitat

Cool, clean stony lakes are the waters in which the Char thrives best, although it is also found in clean rivers.

Spawning

The Char spawns either in November and December or in February and March when the colour of the male is intensified. Yellow eggs measuring 3.5mm in diameter are shed among gravel in either flowing or still water. Those which spawn in the autumn tend to do so in relatively shallow water (not deeper than 3m), but the spring spawners choose deeper water (up to 30m). They mature between four and six years later, the autumn spawners usually maturing more quickly.

Male Humpback salmon in breeding condition (See page 26).

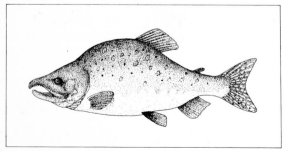

Size

The normal adult length is between 20 and 35cm, while some grow to 40cm. Specimens bigger than this are rare in British waters.

Diet

The Char is wholly carnivorous and eats mainly small crustaceans and insect larvae.

Identification and similar species

The Char is variable in both shape and colour. Usually the back is dark green, brown or black, the sides greenish or bluish orange with yellow or pink spots and the belly is orange or pinkish. The scales are tiny, there being 180 to 240 along the lateral line, the fins are greyish green, black or brown and the lower fins are often red. The vomer is toothed only at the front.

Brook char, S. fontinalis

The back, dorsal and caudal fins of the Brook char are more mottled than those of the Char but the most noticeable differences are the markings on the forward edge of the anal fin which consist of a white stripe with a black stripe adjacent to it. These markings are not present on the Char.

Brown trout, Salmo trutta

The Brown trout has larger scales than the Char, there being 120 to 130 along the lateral line.

Rainbow trout, Salmo gairdneri

The Rainbow trout has a prominent reddish or purple band running from the jaw to the tail and its back and sides, dorsal, adipose and caudal fins are densely spotted with black. It has 120 to 150 scales along the lateral line.

No hybrids involving the Char have been recorded from British waters.

See also plates 9, 10 and 11.

---

12 Char, *Salvelinus alpinus*, male in breeding colours.
Also illustrated: Great northern diver, *Gavia immer*.

In British waters the Coregonidae or whitefishes are confined to a few cool lakes in the north and west and in the case of one species to the North Sea and its estuaries. They are not easy to identify because they all tend to form geographical races as a result of differing local conditions and although most authorities now recognise three British species, at one time many 'species' were accepted as being distinct. This gave rise to the many regional names, some of which are still in use but they merely describe local races of the three species described here.

13 Whitefish

Coregonus lavaretus, Linnaeus 1758

Distribution

The Whitefish is indigenous and although it is common in some waters it is confined to a few lakes in Wales, the Lake District and Scotland.

Habitat
Only large, deep, cool lakes support populations of Whitefish which do not restrict themselves to any particular area of the lake although they do tend to swim deeper than other members of the whitefish family.

Spawning
The Whitefish spawns at any time from October to March with January being the most usual month. Yellow eggs measuring 2.5mm in diameter are laid on stones in still, shallow water and they do not hatch for two months or more when the larvae are 12mm long. They mature between two and three years later when 15 to 20cm in length.

Size
The average adult length is between 20 and 35cm but some specimens reach 40 or 50cm. In lakes where food is scarce dwarf forms can occur which may be mature at around 12cm and which may not exceed 20cm in length.

Diet
The food of the Whitefish consists of free swimming organisms such as water fleas and also bottom living invertebrates and crustaceans.

Identification and similar species
The colour of the back is dark bluish green, the sides are silvery blue and the belly is silvery or white. The fins are usually grey, the colour of the dorsal and caudal fins being darker. There are 80 to 100 scales along the lateral line.
Vendace, C. albula
The Whitefish is usually a little bigger than the Vendace but the best way to separate the two species is to examine the mouth: that of the Whitefish is inferior but that of the Vendace is superior.

No hybrids involving the Whitefish have been recorded from British waters.
See also plate 14.

---

13 Whitefish, *Coregonus lavaretus*.
Also illustrated: Rowan, *Sorbus aucuparia*.

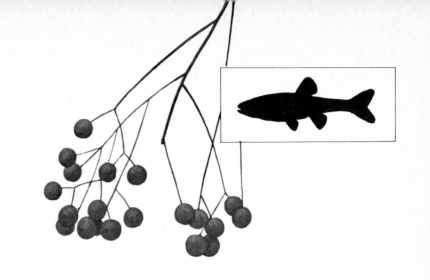

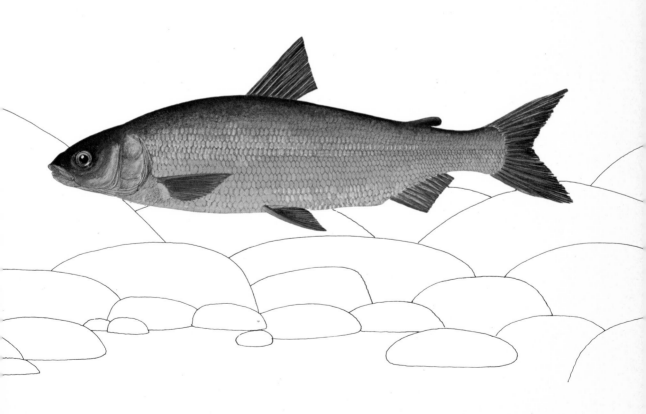

14 Vendace

Coregonus albula, Linnaeus 1758

Distribution

The Vendace is indigenous and although very local it is often found in large numbers in those waters where it does occur. It is confined to the Lake District, southern Scotland and northern and western Ireland.

Habitat

The Vendace is found only in large, deep lakes where it forms shoals in open water but it moves to shallower water to spawn.

Spawning

Spawning takes place in November and December during which time the adults move to the lake margins where yellow eggs measuring just over 2mm in diameter are laid on gravel in still water. They hatch after about three months or more and the larvae immediately move to deeper water. They mature after about three years when they measure between 12 and 16cm in length.

Size

The average length of adult fish is between 15 and 25cm with some specimens reaching 30 or even 35cm.

Diet

The food of the Vendace consists mainly of tiny free swimming organisms such as water fleas but there is some evidence to suggest that during cold weather it feeds on the bottom where invertebrates especially insect larvae are eaten.

Identification and similar species

The colour of the Vendace is silvery blue or whitish on the sides with a darker greenish blue back and a white belly. The fins are greyish and the rear margins of the dorsal and caudal fins are usually a little darker. There are 60 to 70 scales along the lateral line.

Whitefish, C. lavaretus

A few lakes, particularly those in the Lake District, contain populations of both the Vendace and Whitefish and the differences between the two species are given under Whitefish, page 30

No hybrids involving the Vendace have been recorded from British waters.
See also plate 13.

14 Vendace, *Coregonus albula*.
Also illustrated: Water lobelia, *Lobelia dortmanna*.

15 Houting

Coregonus oxyrinchus, Linnaeus 1758

Distribution

The Houting, which is an indigenous species, is rare in British waters and after a decline in its numbers in recent years can best be described as a vagrant. It is likely to be found only in estuaries on the North Sea coast.

Habitat

This is primarily an estuarine species only rarely moving into the open sea but in the spawning season it is found in the lower reaches of rivers and very occasionally in lakes.

Spawning

The Houting ascends rivers in late summer and spawning takes place in the autumn and early winter when yellowish eggs measuring just over 2mm in diameter are shed among gravel or larger stones. As soon as the larvae hatch they swim downstream to coastal waters.

Size

The Houting averages about 25cm in length although specimens as long as 50cm have been recorded.

Diet

The Houting uses its long pointed snout to dig worms and molluscs from the river bed and it also feeds on small free swimming organisms.

Identification

The back is brownish green and the sides and belly are white or silvery. The fins are generally brownish green but often may lack any strong pigment except for the tips of the dorsal and caudal fins which may be blackish. The mouth is inferior and there are 80 to 90 scales along the lateral line.

There are no similar species and no hybrids involving the Houting have been recorded from British waters.

15 Houting, *Coregonus oxyrinchus*.
Also illustrated: Three spined stickleback, *Gasterosteus aculeatus*;
Brackish water crowfoot, *Ranunculus obtusiflorous*.

THYMALLIDAE

Six species of the Thymallidae or graylings occur in Asia, Europe and North America but only one is found in British waters.

16 Grayling

Thymallus thymallus, Linnaeus 1758

Distribution

The Grayling is an indigenous species and is fairly common throughout most of England and Wales and central Scotland.

Habitat

Preferring cool, well oxygenated water the Grayling thrives in moderately fast flowing streams and rivers, typically those below hills. It is non-migratory and is occasionally found in lakes.

Spawning

At the onset of spring when the male has a more boldly marked dorsal fin, large yellow eggs measuring 3.5mm in diameter are deposited on sand and gravel in running water. After fertilisation they are covered with sand and they remain covered until they hatch three or four weeks later. The larvae do not disperse from the spawning area until they are several weeks old and they mature in two to five years when they are 20 to 30cm in length.

Size

Adult Grayling are usually between 25 to 35cm in length although in favourable conditions they grow to 50cm.

Diet

The Grayling is almost entirely carnivorous, the main part of the diet consisting of both water borne and flying insects. The eggs of their own and other species are also eaten and larger specimens take fry and small fish.

Identification

The Grayling has a dark grey back, greyish green or pinkish sides and a white belly. Several longitudinal violet stripes run along the sides and the scales, of which there are 75 to 95 along the lateral line, are faintly hexagonal in shape. There is an adipose fin but by far the most obvious character is the dorsal fin which is very deep and long. It contains 17 to 24 rays and is covered with grey and pink spots. The sides of Grayling in their first year are often marked with parr marks.

There are no similar species and no hybrids involving the Grayling have been recorded from British waters.

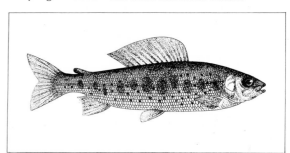

Young Grayling

16 Grayling, *Thymallus thymallus*.
Also illustrated: Orange tip butterfly, *Anthocharis cardamines*;
Water moss, *Fontinalis antipyretica*.

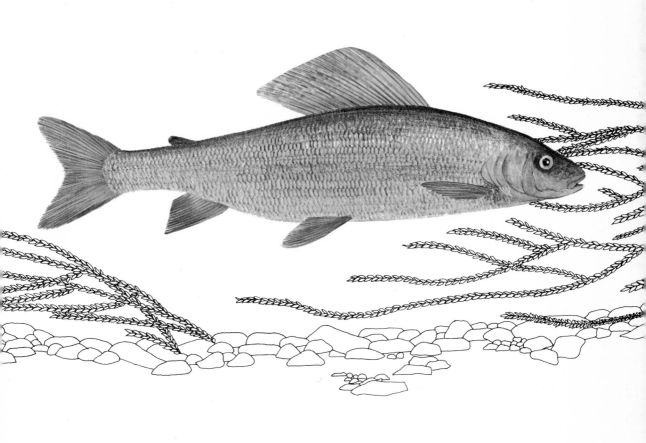

Two members of the Osmeridae are found in Europe but only one occurs in fresh water in Britain.

17 Smelt

Osmerus eperlanus, Linnaeus 1758

Distribution

The Smelt is an indigenous species which spends most of its life in inshore waters and estuaries and enters brackish or occasionally fresh water to spawn. It occurs around most of the coastline of England, Ireland and southern Scotland.

Habitat
The Smelt is found almost exclusively in inshore coastal waters and estuaries, harbours and brackish water. On the mainland of Europe it also occurs in lakes with no access to the sea and while such populations were once known in England they now appear to be extinct.

Spawning
Spawning takes place during March and April in estuaries and the lower reaches of rivers, when small yellowish eggs measuring less than 1mm in diameter are attached to water plants on the river bed. During spawning the males develop small tubercles on the body. The adults return to the sea immediately after the eggs are shed and the larvae hatch between two and four weeks later. They remain close to the spawning grounds until late in the summer, when they measure from 5 to 7cm long.

Size
The usual adult length varies between 10 and 17cm and the Smelt rarely exceeds 20cm.

Diet
Young Smelt feed almost exclusively on invertebrates, taking only a few small fish, but older specimens eat a variety of fish, mainly small inshore shoaling species.

Identification and similar species
The Smelt is an elongate fish with a more or less pointed scaleless head and an adipose fin. The back is greenish, the sides silvery, the belly whitish and the fins are pale grey, the caudal fin usually being a little darker. The lateral line is apparent only on the 9 or 10 scales nearest the head and there are 60 to 66 lateral scales.

Houting, coregonus oxyrinchus
The Smelt superficially resembles all three whitefishes but the Houting is the only member of that family which is found in the same waters as the Smelt, from which it can be distinguished by its protruding snout.

No hybrids involving the Smelt have been recorded from British waters.
See also plate 15.

---

17 Smelt, *Osmerus eperlanus*.
Also illustrated: Egg capsule of Skate, *Raja batis*.

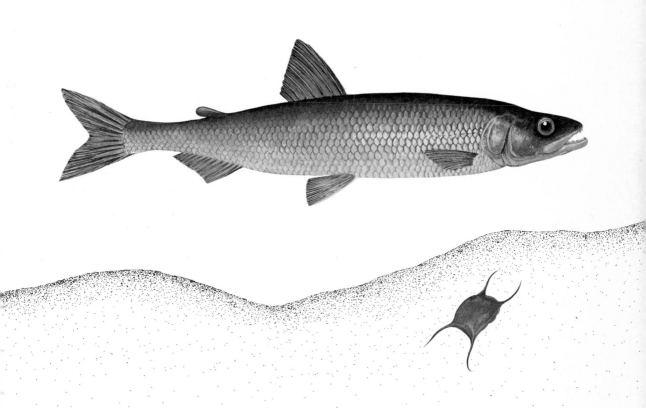

ESOCIDAE

Five species of Esocidae or pike occur throughout Asia, Europe and North America. They all have powerful bodies with long heads and large mouths with strong teeth. Only one species is present in British waters.

18 Pike

Esox lucius, Linnaeus 1758

Distribution

The Pike is widespread throughout the British Isles, being indigenous to England, Scotland and Wales and introduced in Ireland. It is most common in England with the exception of the south west but nowhere on the main islands of Britain is it a scarce fish.

Habitat

The Pike prefers slow flowing or still water and is found in most lakes, canals and lowland rivers where the water is reasonably high in oxygen. Pike do however to a lesser extent occur in faster flowing rivers, but they are generally sedentary and do not swim far from the cover of plants.

Spawning

The breeding season is from February to May when brown eggs measuring from 2.5 to 3mm in diameter are laid among plants to which they adhere. Between one and two weeks later the larvae hatch, remaining among the vegetation until the yolk sac has been absorbed. Only on absorption of the yolk sac does the mouth become fully formed. Growth is normally fast and maturity is reached in two to four years when the fish are 25 to 40cm long.

Size

The adult length is anything between 40 and 100cm, the biggest specimens being females. They live to a considerable age: twenty years is not uncommon.

Diet

Pike feed on invertebrates when young but after two or three months they turn to a diet of fish eggs and fry. Mature Pike eat almost any fish although Roach, *Rutilus rutilus*, Rudd, *Scardinius erythrophthalmus*, and Bleak, *Alburnus alburnus* probably account for most. Amphibians and the young of water fowl are also eaten.

Identification

Although the characteristic shape of the Pike is constant the colour is variable. The back is usually dark green or brown, the sides paler but mottled with dark green, brown or yellow patches or bars. The long head and strong toothed jaws and dorsal and anal fins which are placed well towards the tail make the Pike unmistakable There are 110 to 130 scales along the lateral line.

There are no similar species and no hybrids involving the pike have been recorded from British waters.

18 Pike, *Esox lucius*.
Also illustrated: Ruffe, *Gymnocephalus cernua*; Shining pondweed, *Potamogeton lucens*.

CYPRINIDAE

The Cyprinidae or carp family is the largest family of freshwater fishes occuring in the British Isles. There are sixteen species, five of which have been artificially introduced. They all have a single dorsal fin, all possess scales which are never present on the head and although some species have hardened and sometimes sharp lips, none possess teeth in the jaws. There are within the Cyprinidae some very similar species and hybrids occur more frequently between members of this family than in any other. For this reason pharyngeal bones for each species are illustrated as these are sometimes the only sure way to their identification.

Carp

There are three forms of the Carp found in Britain, the Scaled carp, the Leather carp and the Mirror carp. These three are not separate species, but merely forms of the single species *Cyprinus carpio*. The only real difference between these forms is in the arrangement of the scales. The Scaled carp is uniformly covered with a regular pattern of fairly large scales, the Leather carp is almost devoid of scales and the Mirror carp is partially scaled in one of two types. One type, sometimes known as the Band carp has one row of scales, usually about 40, along the lateral line, another row along the base of the dorsal fin and often a few scales near the anal fin. The second type of Mirror carp has a more random arrangement of scales which are situated on the caudal peduncle, along the base of the dorsal fin, behind the operculum, around the anal, pectoral and pelvic fins and usually, but not always, along the lateral line.

The names for these varieties of Carp have been arrived at rather arbitrarily and while the Scaled carp is usually true to type there is some degree of overlap between the scale arrangements of the Leather carp and Mirror carp with the result that a generously scaled Leather carp could justifiably be referred to as a Mirror carp and vice versa. The various forms of the Carp are the results of selective breeding for food which has gone on in Asia probably for about two thousand years and the original truly wild form from which they stem has a much slimmer body and consequently is of less value as food. In Europe it is restricted to the Danube river system and although it did at one time occur in British waters as an introduced species it has interbred so much with the later introductions of Scaled, Mirror and Leather varieties that it is doubtful if any of the truly wild form remain.

19 Scaled carp

Cyprinus carpio, Linnaeus 1758

Distribution

The Scaled carp which was introduced to Britain in the Middle Ages as a food source is now widespread and common in England although it is less frequent in the north. It does not thrive at high altitudes, is rare in Scotland, uncommon in most of Wales and is thinly scattered in Ireland.

Habitat

All Carp thrive in rich weedy lakes, ponds, canals and slow flowing rivers. They can tolerate water where the oxygen content is low, tend to form small shoals and although they generally swim near the bottom, on warm summer days they often bask lazily near the surface.

Spawning

Between May and July yellow eggs measuring nearly 1.5mm in diameter are shed onto plants in standing or slow moving water. Spawning usually takes place at the edges of the water and consequently the plants chosen are often Reed, *Phragmites communis* and Reedmace, *Typha*

Original wild form of the Carp

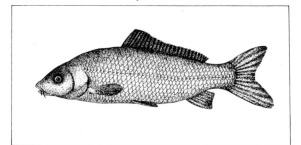

19 Scaled carp, *Cyprinus carpio*.
Also illustrated: Great duckweed, *Lemna polyrrhiza*; Fennel leaved pondweed, *Potamogeton pectinatus*.

latifolia. The eggs hatch in about a week and the larvae which are 5mm long on hatching remain among the plants, feeding off their yolk sacs for up to ten days. They grow very quickly reaching a length of 14cm in a year, 25cm in two years, 30cm in three years, and they mature between three and four years later when 30 to 35cm long. Carp have a long life and although some estimates are excessively optimistic they certainly live to fifteen years and possibly to twenty years in the wild, while in captivity they may live twice as long. They probably would not have spread so widely throughout Britain if it were not for this longevity as these islands are rather too far north to provide ideal spawning conditions, and populations of carp do not enjoy great breeding success in poor summers.

Size

Adult Scaled carp average between 25 and 50cm in length, the larger specimens usually being females, but as they pass their prime they tend to lose weight and become more sluggish.

Diet

All Carp are omnivorous. The very young fish feed almost entirely on tiny free swimming organisms, but after about six months they move to the bottom for their food which consists of insect larvae and worms, and later molluscs and crustaceans are added to the diet. Plants are eaten especially in the summer, while in winter feeding becomes more intermittent and in very cold weather may cease altogether.

Identification and similar species

The Scaled carp has a deep body which is covered with large scales. The dorsal fin is long, containing 17 to 22 branched rays, and there are four barbels, two each side of the relatively small mouth. The back is usually greenish brown, the sides yellowish brown usually with a golden tinge, the belly is creamy yellow and all the fins are yellowish brown although the caudal fin can sometimes be blackish while the anal and pelvic fins may have a slight red tinge. There are 33 to 40 scales along the lateral line.

An ornamental form has been bred where the body is coloured orange or golden.

Crucian carp, Carassius carassius

The Crucian carp is smaller and is usually deeper in the body than the Scaled carp but the positive difference between the two species is that the Crucian carp has no barbels.

Hybrids

All forms of the Carp hybridise freely with the Crucian carp and the offspring are generally intermediate between the parents.

See also plates 20, 21, 22 and 56.

20 Leather carp

Cyprinus carpio, Linnaeus 1758

Distribution

The Leather carp which is an introduced species occurs in those places where the Scaled carp is found, although it is probably not so common nor does it tend to be found so far north.

Habitat, spawning, size and diet

See under Scaled carp.

Identification

The Leather carp possesses the same physical features as the Scaled carp except that it has virtually no scales save for a few which are usually close to the bases of the fins especially the anal fin. Occasionally Leather carp may be entirely devoid of scales and usually the colouration is browner than that of the Scaled carp. There are no similar species.

Hybrids

See under Scaled carp.

Pharyngeal bone

---

20 Leather carp, *Cyprinus carpio*.
Also illustrated: Mute swan, *Cygnus olor*; Perfoliate pondweed, *Potamogeton perfoliatus*.

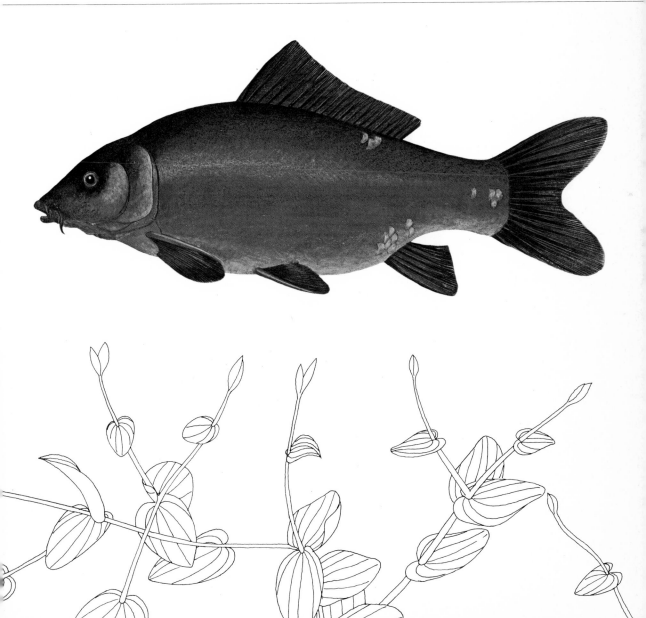

21 Mirror carp

Cyprinus carpio, Linnaeus 1758

Distribution

The Mirror carp which is an introduced species is found in the same areas as the Scaled carp although it is rather more common.

Habitat and spawning

See under Scaled carp.

Size

The Mirror carp is very similar in size to the Scaled carp and Leather carp but it tends to grow more quickly and often reaches a greater size than the other two forms.

Diet

See under Scaled carp.

Identification

The Mirror carp occurs in the two types which are described in the general introduction to carp on page 42 and there are no similar species.

Hybrids

See under Scaled carp.

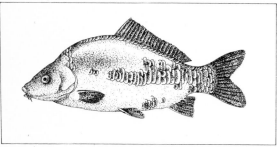

Typical example of the form of the Mirror carp where the scales are situated mainly on the caudal peduncle, along the base of the dorsal fin and in a random manner along the lateral line

21 Mirror carp, *Cyprinus carpio*.
Also illustrated: Yew, *Taxus baccata*.

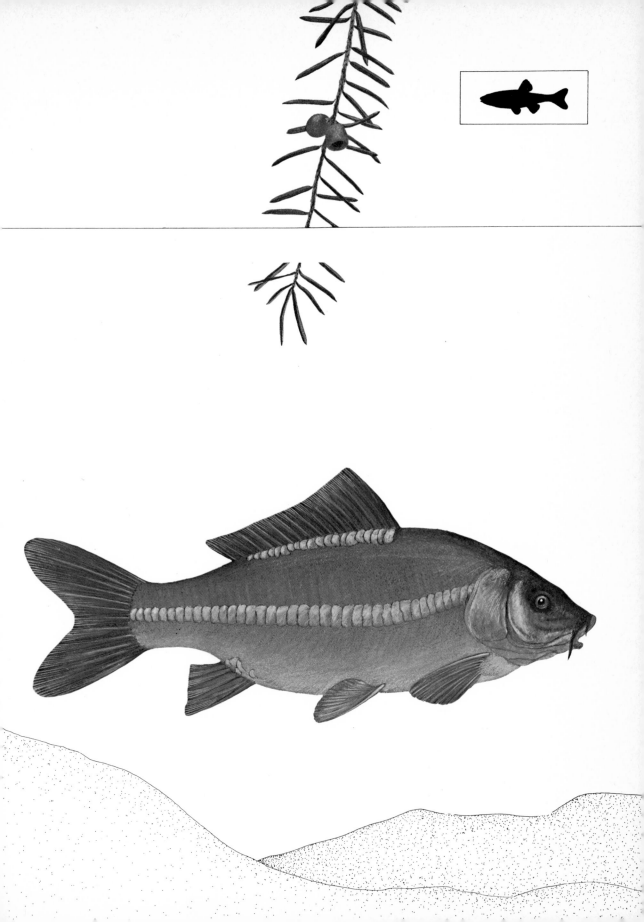

22 Crucian carp

Carassius carassius, Linnaeus 1758

Distribution

The Crucian carp is locally common throughout England and Wales and is most frequently encountered in the south east of England and East Anglia but it is absent from Ireland and Scotland. It was considered to be a fairly recently introduced species until 1975 when the discovery of a Crucian carp bone among Roman remains in London pointed to the fact that it is an indigenous species or at least a very early introduction.

Habitat

The Crucian carp is essentially a fish of rich, even overgrown lakes, canals and slow flowing rivers. It tends to spend most of its time near the bottom, can thrive in waters with a low oxygen content, and often becomes torpid in cold weather.

Spawning

In May and June the Crucian carp lays yellowish or orange eggs measuring 1.5mm in diameter among the vegetation in overgrown areas of shallow water. The eggs adhere to the plants and hatch in six to twelve days when the larvae measure about 5mm. Growth is variable being slow in overgrown or small ponds, but quicker in lakes which have areas of open water. The average length at maturity (between three and four years) is about 10 or 11cm.

Size

The Crucian carp is rarely as big as the Carp, commonly reaching up to 25cm in length and occasionally up to 40 or 50cm.

Diet

The Crucian carp feeds mainly on invertebrates, especially insect larvae and also on plants.

Identification and similar species

The Crucian carp is a deep bodied fish which is variable in body shape and has a small mouth with no barbels. The back is greenish brown, the sides yellowish brown usually with a slight golden tinge and the belly is pale yellow or orange. The fins are brownish and there is usually a golden or reddish tint on the pelvic, pectoral and anal fins. There are 31 to 36 scales along the lateral line. As well as the normal form illustrated a smaller big headed form occurs in overcrowded waters, and where food and space are plentiful, an excessively deep bodied form develops. A variety of body shapes are known between these two extremes.

Carp, Cyprinus carpio
The Crucian carp can be separated from the Carp by the absence of barbels around its mouth.

Goldfish, Carassius auratus
The differences between the Crucian carp and the Goldfish are given under Goldfish, page 50.

Hybrids
Hybrids between the Crucian carp and the Carp are relatively common.

See also plates 19, 23 and 56.

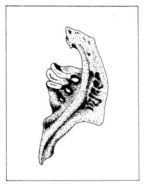

Pharyngeal bone

---

22 Crucian carp, *Carassius carassius*.
Also illustrated: Orange foxtail grass, *Alopecurus aequalis*.

23 Goldfish

Carassius auratus, Linnaeus 1758

Distribution

The Goldfish which was introduced to Britain from Eastern Europe is widely distributed but uncommon in England, rare in Scotland and Wales and absent from Ireland.

Habitat

The Goldfish is tolerant of conditions in which many other fish would perish. It is its ability to survive in small, often oxygen deficient ponds which has made it an ideal aquarium fish. In the wild state in Britain it is usually found in canals and ponds with abundant plant growth.

Spawning

The Goldfish spawns in summer when yellow eggs measuring 1.5mm in diameter are attached to plants. The larvae which are brownish in colour hatch in about a week and they do not assume the reddish golden colour of the adults until over a year old. As this species needs relatively warm water in which to spawn it is likely that the population would be rather smaller than it is if it were not from time to time added to by escapes from captivity, although populations would probably be stable in waters which are artificially warmed by waste water from power stations and other industrial plants.

Size

Goldfish grow to 30cm or rarely 40cm in length but the usual adult length is nearer 20cm.

Diet

The food of the Goldfish consists mainly of a wide variety of invertebrates but this diet is supplemented from time to time by plant matter.

Identification and similar species

The colouration of the Goldfish is variable. Usually the back is reddish brown to olive, the sides orange or golden brown and the belly yellow or silver. The scales are large and the longest rays of both the dorsal and anal fins are serrated. All the fins are orange or golden brown and there are no barbels around the mouth. Some specimens never attain the characteristic golden colour and retain the brownish hue of immature fish. There are 27 to 33 scales along the lateral line.

Crucian carp, Carassius carassius

The Goldfish and the Crucian carp are very similar in appearance; indeed some authorities regard them as varieties of the same species but the Goldfish has a less deep body than the Crucian carp and the serrations on the rays of the dorsal and anal fins of the Crucian carp are far less pronounced than those of the Goldfish. The Crucian carp has 31 to 36 scales along the lateral line. Many strange, even grotesque forms of the Goldfish are kept in aquaria and those which escape soon perish or revert to the form described here. They are occasionally found but are not separate species.

No hybrids involving the Goldfish have been recorded from British waters.
See also plate 22.

Pharyngeal bone

---

23 Goldfish, *Carassius auratus*.
Also illustrated: Blackberry, *Rubus fruticosus*.

24 Tench

Tinca tinca, Linnaeus 1758

Distribution

The Tench is indigenous and common in England and Wales although it is thinly scattered in the north and west. It is scarce in Scotland and locally common in Ireland.

Habitat

Lakes, canals and slow flowing rivers which are rich in vegetation provide ideal conditions for the Tench. It is capable of existing in waters with a low oxygen content and may become torpid in severe winters remaining on or in the bottom mud.

Spawning

The Tench spawns from May to July in still water when yellowish eggs measuring about 1mm in diameter are deposited among vegetation to which they adhere although they may occasionally be left on the bottom. The larvae which hatch in about a week grow slowly, reaching only about 3 to 4cm after one year. They mature between 10 and 15cm in length when three or four years old.

Size

The normal average length is between 20 and 30cm although the Tench can grow to 50 or exceptionally 60cm.

Diet

A wide variety of bottom living animals is eaten including molluscs and particularly the larvae of insects. Although young specimens eat algae, plant food forms only a low percentage of the diet of mature fish.

Identification

The Tench has a dark back which is almost black in colour, dark greyish green sides with a pale olive green belly usually with an orange or bronze tinge which is intensified on the males during spawning. All the fins are dark, often being almost black, the iris is red and there is one small barbel at either side of the mouth. The scales are small, there being 95 to 120 along the lateral line and the skin is very slimy. The pelvic fins of the male are much longer than those of the female.

A golden variety of the Tench is commonly kept in ornamental ponds.

There are no similar species and no hybrids involving the Tench have been recorded from British waters.

Pharyngeal bone

24 Tench, *Tinca tinca*.
Also illustrated: Shining pondweed, *Potamogeton lucens*.

25 Gudgeon

Gobio gobio, Linnaeus 1758

Distribution

The Gudgeon is fairly widespread and it is common and even abundant in some areas. It is indigenous and occurs throughout the British Isles, being most common in England and scarce in Scotland.

Habitat

Typically a fish of fairly fast flowing streams with sandy or gravelly bottoms, the Gudgeon is also found in ponds and lakes. It often forms shoals, and is always found on or near the bottom.

Spawning

Spawning takes place over an extended period from April to July but is most intense during May and June when the male develops white tubercles on the head. The eggs which are clear, yellowish or sometimes slightly bluish measure just under 2mm in diameter and are shed among plants or stones to which they adhere. They hatch from two to three weeks later and reach maturity after three years.

Size

The Gudgeon rarely grows to more than 20cm long, the usual adult length being from 10 to 15cm.

Diet

The food of the Gudgeon tends to vary with the seasons, but is almost entirely animal. In spring and summer it eats mostly insects and their larvae, while in the autumn and winter it turns to a diet of molluscs and crustaceans. Some plant matter is also eaten.

Identification and similar species

The Gudgeon is a small fish with a fairly long snout and one barbel at each corner of the mouth. The back is brown, the sides are pale brown or greenish yellow and there is a row of about eight darker rounded spots running from head to tail. These spots however are usually rather indistinct and sometimes absent altogether. The belly is silvery, greyish or yellow and the fins are pale brown, the dorsal and caudal fins being black spotted. There are 38 to 44 scales along the lateral line.

Barbel, Barbus barbus
Gudgeon superficially resemble small Barbel but they have two barbels around the mouth as opposed to the Barbel's four.

No hybrids involving the Gudgeon have been recorded from British waters.
See also plate 26.

Pharyngeal bone

---

25 Gudgeon, *Gobio gobio*.
Also illustrated: Grey heron, *Ardea cinerea*; Canadian pondweed, *Elodea canadensis*.

26 Barbel

Barbus barbus, Linnaeus 1758

Distribution

The Barbel is indigenous and widespread throughout England but is absent from Ireland, Scotland and most of Wales. Its distribution in England has been extended in the interests of angling: for instance the Severn river system which is now fairly rich in Barbel once contained none.

Habitat

The Barbel prefers clear, deep, stony rivers and is typically a fish of large, moderately fast flowing waters with beds of sand.

Spawning

Spawning takes place from May to July. There is something of an upstream migration to the spawning grounds where yellow eggs measuring 2mm in diameter are shed in running water over sandy shallows. They hatch in about two weeks and the Barbel matures in four to five years.

Size

The Barbel is a powerful fish and grows to a length of up to 80cm. The usual adult length however is between 30 and 50cm.

Diet

Feeding usually at night on the bottom, the Barbel consumes insect larvae, molluscs, crustaceans and worms and occasionally it eats small fish and some plant matter.

Identification and similar species

The Barbel is a long bodied fish with a pointed snout which has four barbels around the mouth. The longest ray of the dorsal fin is sharply serrated and there are between 55 and 65 scales along the lateral line. The colour is variable but tends to be greyish brown on the back while the sides are greenish with a golden tinge and the belly is creamy white. The fins are greyish and there is often a pink tint to the pelvic, pectoral and anal fins.

Gudgeon, Gobio gobio
The Gudgeon is similar in body shape to the Barbel but is very much smaller and has only two barbels around the mouth.

Pharyngeal bone

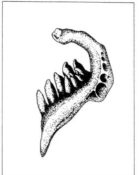

No hybrids involving the Barbel have been recorded from British waters.
See also plate 25.

26 Barbel, *Barbus barbus*.
Also illustrated: Shell of Ramshorn pond snail, *Planorbis planorbis*; Shining pondweed, *Potamogeton lucens*.

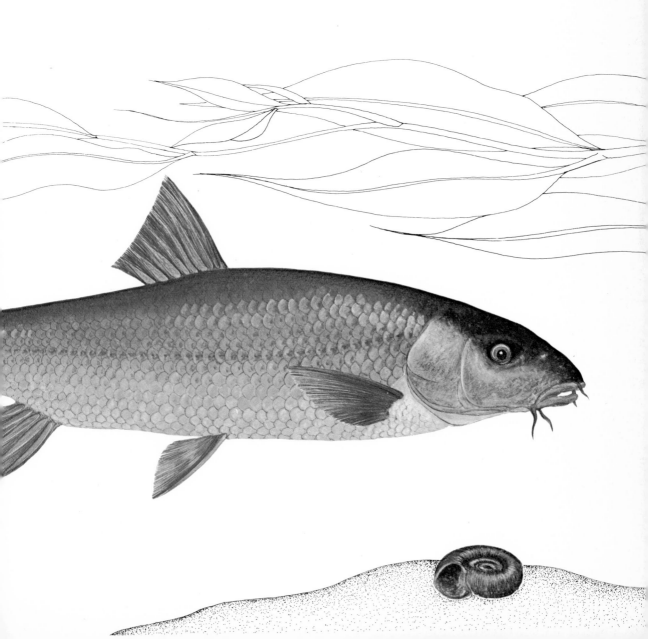

27 Bream

Abramis brama, Linnaeus 1758

Distribution

The Bream is indigenous to Britain. It is common throughout most of England although it is local in the south west. It is less common in Wales, confined to the south of Scotland and is fairly widespread in Ireland.

Habitat

The Bream is found only in still or slow flowing waters, usually in lakes or rivers with a muddy bottom. It is rather a shy fish and forms large shoals especially in winter when it frequents deeper water.

Spawning

In May and June the males develop conspicuous pale tubercles on the head and back and amid the cover of vegetation the female lays yellow eggs measuring 1.5mm in diameter which adhere to the plants. In warm weather they hatch within a few days but usually hatching takes over a week. Once the larvae have absorbed their yolk sacs they form shoals and begin feeding on minute animals and plants. Bream grow fairly slowly and do not reach maturity until they are about eight years old when they are 25 to 30cm long.

Size

The normal adult length is between 25 and 45cm although larger specimens often occur and Bream between 50 and 60cm are by no means rare.

Diet

Most small organisms found in the bottom mud are eaten, especially worms and the larvae of insects. The Bream is able to extend its mouth to form a sucking tube and adopts an almost vertical position when feeding.

Identification and similar species

The Bream has a deep slimy body with a long concave anal fin which contains 23 to 29 branched rays. The back is usually deep brown, the sides yellowish brown and the belly silver or white but there are many colour variations from silver to almost black. There are 50 to 60 scales along the lateral line.

Silver Bream, Blicca bjoerkna

Pale specimens of the Bream can usually be distinguished from the Silver Bream by the fact that the eye of the Bream is comparatively smaller than that of the Silver Bream. In addition, the Bream has 11 to 15 scales between the dorsal fin and the lateral line while the Silver Bream has 8 to 11.

Hybrids

The Bream hybridises with Roach, *Rutilus rutilus*, Rudd, *Scardinius erythrophthalmus* and Orfe, *Leuciscus idus* and without very detailed examination there is no reliable way to identification.

See also plates 28, 57 and 58.

Pharyngeal bone

---

27 Bream, *Abramis brama*.
Also illustrated: Larva of Silver water beetle, *Hydrous piceus*;
Broad leaved pondweed, *Potamogeton natans*.

28 Silver bream

Blicca bjoerkna, Linnaeus 1758

Distribution

The indigenous Silver bream is locally common in parts of England, particularly the eastern Midlands. It is scarce north of Yorkshire, rare in Wales and absent from Ireland and Scotland.

Habitat

The Silver bream inhabits canals, lakes and slow flowing rivers which are rich in vegetation.

Spawning

Between May and July the males develop pale spawning tubercles on the head and front part of the body. Yellowish eggs measuring about 2mm in diameter are deposited by the female among dense plants to which they adhere. They hatch in five to eight days when the larvae measure nearly 5mm in length, and mature three or four years later when they measure from 10 to 13cm.

Size

The average length of adults is 20 to 25cm but in a good environment they may reach 35cm.

Diet

The food of the Silver bream is very similar to that of the Bream, *Abramis brama* and consists mainly of small bottom living animals supplemented by algae and other plant matter. It is unable to protrude its mouth when feeding as the Bream does and it barely feeds at all in the winter.

Identification and similar species

The Silver bream is a deep bodied fish; the eye is large and the long anal fin contains 21 to 23 branched rays. The back is greyish or brownish green, the sides silvery, the belly white and the fins are grey but the pelvic fins are usually tinted with red. There are 44 to 48 scales along the lateral line.

Bream, Abramis brama
For the difference between Bream and Silver bream see under Bream, page 58.

No hybrids involving the Silver bream have been recorded from British waters.
See also plate 27.

Pharyngeal bone

---

28 Silver bream, *Blicca bjoerkna*.
Also illustrated: Red admiral butterfly, *Vanessa atalanta*.

29 Bleak

Alburnus alburnus, Linnaeus 1758

Distribution

The indigenous Bleak is locally common throughout England, especially in the east. It is absent from Ireland and Scotland and scarce in Wales.

Habitat

The Bleak favours clear lakes and rivers and tends to form shoals near the surface but in the winter it inhabits deeper water.

Spawning

Between April and June the males develop white tubercles on the head and the lower fins become tinted with red. The eggs which are yellowish and measure 1.5mm in diameter are shed in very shallow water and adhere to plants and stones. They hatch from two to three weeks later when the larvae are about 3mm long, reach a length of from 3 to 5cm after a year and mature in two to three years at 7 or 8cm.

Size

The usual adult length is from 10 to 15cm and Bleak occasionally grow to 20cm.

Diet

The Bleak feeds almost entirely on small invertebrates, usually those which inhabit open water although it does feed on the bottom to some extent.

Identification

The Bleak is a small, slender fish with a dark bluish grey back and silvery sides and belly. The mouth is superior and the fins are pale grey or white. There are from 46 to 53 scales along the lateral line and 18 to 23 rays in the anal fin. There are no similar species.

Hybrids

The Bleak hybridises with Chub, *Leuciscus cephalus*, Dace, *L. leuciscus* and Roach, *Rutilus rutilus* and the resulting offspring are variable and difficult to identify.

See also plates 57, 59 and 60.

Pharyngeal bone

29 Bleak, *Alburnus alburnus*.

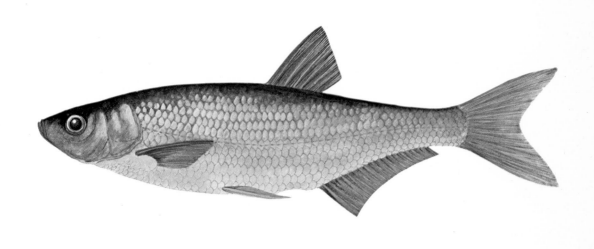

30 Minnow

Phoxinus phoxinus, Linnaeus 1758

Distribution

The Minnow is indigenous and is common throughout the British Isles with the exception of northern Scotland where it occurs less frequently than in other areas.

Habitat

Clear stony rivers, streams and lakes provide ideal conditions for the Minnow although it will live in ponds so long as they are not too muddy. During the summer it tends to form shoals near the surface but in colder weather these shoals break up and individual fish swim closer to the bottom, sometimes seeking refuge beneath stones.

Spawning

Between April and June the male develops a bright red tint on the belly and white tubercles on the head. Pale yellow eggs measuring 1.5mm in diameter are laid among stones in running water and they hatch in a little under a week. The fry which remain among the stones until the yolk sac is absorbed measure about 5mm in length. Growth is variable and they mature in one or two years.

Size

Mature minnows are usually between 6 and 12cm long while the normal maximum length is around 10cm.

Diet

The diet of the minnow is diverse and although some algae and other plant matter is consumed the species is in the main predatory and takes a wide variety of invertebrates especially insects and their larvae.

Identification

The Minnow is a small, sleek fish with very small scales and an incomplete lateral line which is not present on the caudal peduncle. The colour is variable but usually the back is dark brown, the upper sides olive brown fading into yellowish brown below and the belly is silvery grey. There is a row of more or less round or elongated darker patches on each side and these may be fused together to form an irregular stripe. There are 85 to 100 lateral scales.

There are no similar species and no hybrids involving the Minnow have been recorded from British waters.

Pharyngeal bone

30 Minnow, *Phoxinus phoxinus*, male in breeding colours (top), and female (bottom).
Also illustrated: Great pond snail, *Limnaea stagnalis*; Small bur reed, *Sparganium minimum*.

31 Bitterling

Rhodeus sericeus, Bloch 1782

Distribution

The Bitterling which is an introduced species is very local and rare. It is likely that the known colonies in Shropshire, Cheshire and Lancashire are the result of escapes from aquaria. It was discovered living wild in the first quarter of this century and is not yet known to be established in any other area in the British Isles: indeed, it appears to be decreasing in numbers.

Habitat

The Bitterling is found in small, sandy lakes and to a lesser extent in canals and slow flowing rivers where mussels of the family Unionidae occur.

Spawning

From May to July the males develop an intense purple colour on the body, white tubercles on the head and red dorsal and anal fins, while the females develop a long ovipositor. By means of this the yellowish eggs which measure 3mm in diameter are laid in the mantle cavities of the Swan mussel, *Anodonta cygnaea*, and other bivalves and the shed sperm from the male is taken in by the mussel as it respires. Several eggs are laid in one mussel and the larvae emerge through the inhalant syphon three or four weeks later when they have consumed their yolk sacs and measure 2cm in length.

Size

The Bitterling is a small fish which averages between 5 and 8cm in length and which is rarely longer than 10cm.

Diet

Small invertebrates make up most of the Bitterling's diet but a little plant matter is also eaten.

Identification

The Bitterling is a deep bodied fish which has a bluish grey back, paler blue or silvery sides and a white belly. The lateral line is restricted to between 4 and 7 scales nearest the head and there are 34 to 38 lateral scales. There is a bright metallic blue horizontal stripe on the caudal peduncle and the fins are pale grey often tinted with orange.

There are no similar species and no hybrids involving the Bitterling have been recorded from British waters.

Pharyngeal bone

31 Bitterling, *Rhodeus sericeus*, male (top), and female (bottom), in breeding condition.
Also illustrated: Canadian pondweed, *Elodea canadensis*.

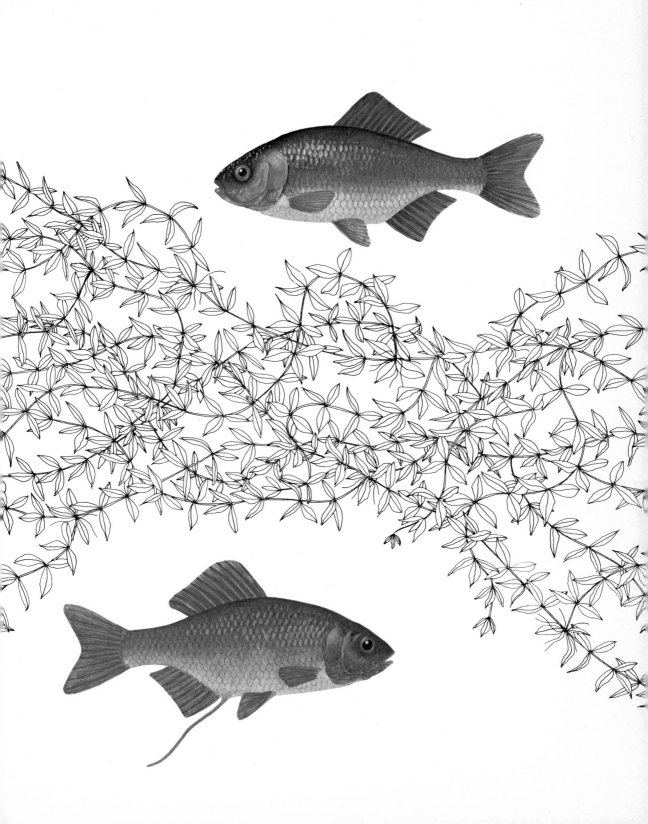

32 Rudd

Scardinius erythrophthalmus, Linnaeus 1758

Distribution

An indigenous species, the Rudd is widespread but
absent from most of Scotland. It is most frequent in the
south and east of England.

Habitat

The Rudd thrives amongst vegetation in lowland lakes,
slow flowing rivers and canals and is often found in waters
which have become neglected and are overgrown. It
swims in small shoals often keeping company with Roach,
Rutilus rutilus and Bream, *Abramis brama*. In summer it
frequents shallow water but in winter it is found in deeper
pools.

Spawning

In May and June yellow eggs measuring 1.5mm in
diameter are laid which adhere to the leaves of water
plants. The larvae hatch in one to two weeks and they
feed on minute animals when the yolk sac has been
absorbed. They turn to a mainly vegetable diet when
about a year old and 7 to 9cm in length, maturing in two
to three years when about 12cm in length.

Size

Although usually a little larger than its near relation the
Roach, the Rudd rarely exceeds 35cm in length and the
adults normally measure 15 to 30cm.

Diet

The food of the Rudd is very similar to that of the Roach
and includes invertebrates and some plant matter but it
tends to feed closer to the surface than the Roach.

Identification and similar species

The Rudd is a deep bodies fish with a dark brownish
green back, golden yellow sides and a white belly. The
pelvic, anal and caudal fins are more or less red, there are
40 to 45 scales along the lateral line, and the iris is golden.

Roach, Rutilus rutilus

The origin of the dorsal fin of the Roach is above the base
of the pelvic fins whereas that of the Rudd is nearer the
tail. The mouth of the Rudd is more or less superior while
that of the Roach tends to be inferior. There is usually
more red in the fins of the Rudd and more yellow in its
body and the iris of the Roach is red.

Hybrids

The Rudd hybridises freely with Roach and Bream and
also with Dace, *Leuciscus leuciscus* and the resulting
offspring are variable and difficult to identify.

See also plates 33, 58, 59 and 60.

Pharyngeal bone

---

32 Rudd, *Scardinius erythrophthalmus*.
Also illustrated: Small bur reed, *Sparganium minimum*.

33 Roach

Rutilus rutilus, Linnaeus 1758

Distribution

The indigenous Roach is very common in England except for the extreme south west where it is local. It is also local in Wales and Ireland and does not occur in northern Scotland. Large numbers of Roach were affected by the epidemic known as Ulcerative Dermal Necrosis in the 1960s but in most areas populations have made up their numbers.

Habitat

The Roach naturally inhabits rich lowland lakes, and slow flowing rivers where it collects in shoals which may also contain Rudd, *Scardinius erythrophthalmus*, Bream, *Abramis brama* and other members of the Cyprinidae. It has however been introduced to other waters in the interests of angling and is now found in almost all types of lowland waters.

Spawning

The Roach spawns in April, May and sometimes June when the males develop white tubercles on the head and fins. Yellow eggs measuring between 1 and 1.5mm in diameter are shed amongst dense vegetation to which they adhere. They hatch in about ten days and the larvae which are between 6 and 7mm long remain among the plants for several days. They mature between two and four years later.

Size

The average length of adult Roach is 15 to 25cm although they quite commonly grow to 30cm.

Diet

The Roach eats both invertebrates and plant matter and feeds mainly on the bottom. It eats less in the winter and fasts entirely during spawning.

Identification and similar species

The colouration is variable but usually the back is dark bluish green, the sides bluish or silvery and the belly is white. The dorsal and caudal fins are greyish brown, the lower fins especially the pelvic and anal fins are reddish, and the iris is red. The origin of the dorsal fin is above the base of the pelvic fins and there are 42 to 45 scales along the lateral line.

Rudd, Scardinius erythrophthalmus
The differences between Roach and Rudd are given under Rudd, page 68.
Hybrids
The Roach hybridises freely with Rudd and Bream and also with Bleak, *Alburnus alburnus* and the offspring are variable and difficult to identify.

See also plates 32, 57 and 59.

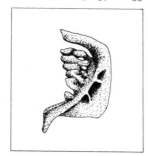

Pharyngeal bone

33 Roach, *Rutilus rutilus*.
Also illustrated: Water shrew, *Neomys fodiens*; Whorled water milfoil, *Myriophyllum verticillatum*.

34 Chub

Leuciscus cephalus, Linnaeus 1758

Distribution

The Chub is widely distributed in England, except for the extreme south west, is scarce in west Wales and southern Scotland and absent from Ireland and central and northern Scotland.

Habitat

The Chub is typically a fish of the middle reaches of rivers where the water is deep, clean and flows fairly quickly. It is also found in the lower reaches of rivers and occasionally in lakes. Young Chub are gregarious and form shoals, but older specimens are solitary and may become territorial.

Spawning

The Chub spawns between April and June when it seeks sheltered water to shed its eggs on to plants. The eggs are yellowish, measure 1.5 to 2mm in diameter and hatch in about a week when the larvae measure from 5 to 7mm in length. Growth is slow and after a year they do not measure more than 4cm, but later they grow more quickly and mature between three and five years when from 18 to 22cm long.

Size

One of the larger Cyprinids, the Chub grows to a length of 50 or even 60cm but it does not normally exceed 45cm.

Diet

The Chub is omnivorous. Fish probably form the largest constituent of the diet of large specimens but they also take a variety of plant matter and invertebrates.

Identification and similar species

The Chub has a dark greyish green back, grey, greenish or bluish sides with a silver or golden sheen on its large scales and a yellowish belly. The head is broad, the body elongate, the mouth terminal and large and the pectoral, dorsal, and caudal fins are dark brown while the pelvic and anal fins are reddish brown. There are 44 to 46 scales along the lateral line.

Dace, L. leuciscus
The Dace has more than 46 scales along the lateral line and the anal fin has a concave edge, whereas the Chub has less than 46 scales along the lateral line and a convex edge to the anal fin.

Orfe, L. idus
The Orfe has more than 54 scales along the lateral line and while the edge of its anal fin is sometimes almost straight, it is never convex.

Hybrids
The Chub hybridises with the Bleak, *Alburnus alburnus* and the offspring are variable and not easy to identify.

See also plates 35, 36 and 57.
For illustration of pharyngeal bone see page 74.

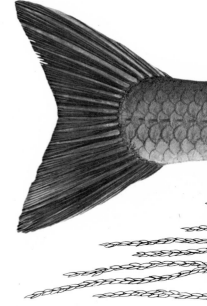

A far eastern species, the Grass carp, *Ctenopharyngodon idella* which superficially resembles the Chub is present under strict supervision in a few waters in Britain. It has been introduced experimentally in an attempt to evaluate its potential as a controller of plant growth. A vegetarian, it eats voraciously and in its natural habitat grows to a length of 80cm. It is yellowish brown in colour, has greyish brown fins and the mouth is inferior. There are usually 43 to 45 scales along the lateral line, 7 branched rays in the dorsal fin and 8 branched rays in the anal fin. It is most unlikely to be found and, being a warm water species, would probably not breed successfully if released into the wild.

34 Chub, *Leuciscus cephalus*.
Also illustrated: Water moss, *Fontinalis antipyretica*.

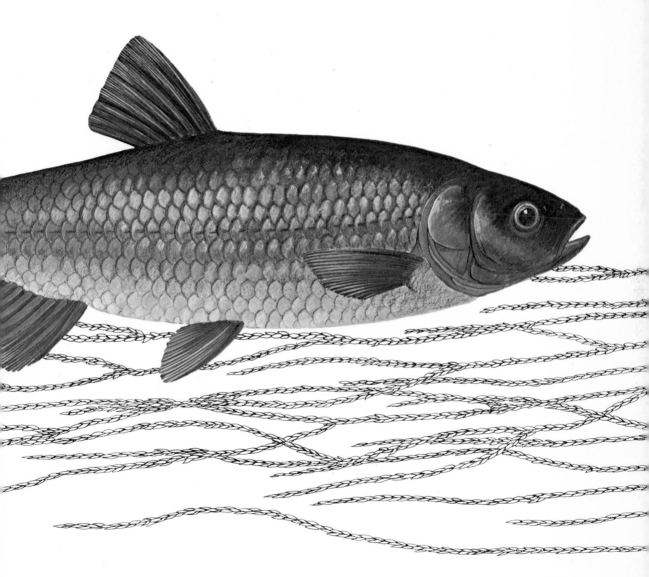

35 Orfe

Leuciscus idus, Linnaeus 1758

Distribution

Pharyngeal bone

The Orfe has been introduced from the mainland of Europe to a few British waters, mostly in the south of England where it is widespread but uncommon.

Habitat

In winter the Orfe is found in the deeper parts of lakes and slow flowing rivers but in the spring it migrates to shallower water to spawn, where it remains throughout the summer.

Spawning

Yellow eggs measuring 1.5mm in diameter are laid between April and July in still or slow flowing water and are attached to plants, stones or submerged roots. The larvae hatch after about a fortnight and the Orfe reaches maturity between four and six years later when measuring 15 to 20cm in length.

Size

The normal adult length is between 25 and 30cm but in waters which are relatively free from predators the Orfe, which can live for up to twenty years, attains lengths of 40cm or more.

Diet

The food consists of a wide variety of invertebrates including bottom living snails, insect larvae and flying insects.

Identification and similar species

The Orfe has a dark greyish green back with paler sides and a silvery belly. The pelvic and anal fins are reddish brown and the iris is usually more or less yellow. There are 56 to 61 scales along the lateral line.

A yellow or golden variety of the Orfe is often kept in ornamental ponds.

Chub, L. cephalus

The differences between the Chub and the Orfe are given under Chub, page 72.

Dace, L. leuciscus

The Dace is a more slender fish than the Orfe and the origin of its dorsal fin which has a concave edge is more or less above the base of the pelvic fins. The origin of the dorsal fin of the Orfe which has a convex or only slightly concave edge is situated behind the base of the pelvic fins. The Dace has 49 to 52 scales along the lateral line.

Hybrids

The Orfe occasionally hybridises with the Bream, *Abramis brama* and the rarely encountered offspring are more or less intermediate between the parents but do vary and consequently are difficult to identify.

See also plates 34, 36 and 58.

Pharyngeal bone of Chub (page 72)

35 Orfe, *Leuciscus idus*.
Also illustrated: Duckweed, *Lemna minor*; Horned pondweed, *Zannichellia palustris*.

36 Dace

Leuciscus leuciscus, Linnaeus 1758

Distribution

The indigenous Dace is locally common throughout England except the extreme south west where it is scarce. It is local in east Wales but rare in west Wales and it is found only in the south of both Ireland and Scotland.

Habitat

The Dace is found in cool streams and rivers and rarely in lakes. It often swims in shoals near the surface.

Spawning

Spawning takes place from March to May in running water when the males develop white tubercles on the head and body. The yellow eggs which measure 1.5mm in diameter are attached to plants and they hatch in two to three weeks when the larvae are about 7mm long. They grow quickly and mature between one and two years when 12 to 15cm long.

Size

The Dace exceptionally reaches a length of 30cm but the usual adult length is 15 to 25cm.

Diet

Large numbers of flying insects are eaten, especially during summer, in addition to aquatic insects, molluscs, crustaceans and some plant matter.

Identification and similar species

The Dace is a slender fish with a smallish head and no barbels. The back is dark greyish green, the sides silvery green and the belly is white. The dorsal and caudal fins are usually greyish green while the lower fins are greenish yellow often tinted with pink. The iris is yellowish and there are 49 to 52 scales along the lateral line.

Chub, L. cephalus
The differences between Chub and Dace are given under Chub, page 72.

Orfe, L. idus
The differences between the Dace and the Orfe are given under Orfe, page 74.

Hybrids
The Dace hybridises with both the Bleak, *Alburnus alburnus* and the Rudd, *Scardinius erythrophthalmus* and the offspring are variable and not easy to identify.

See also plates 34, 35 and 60.

Pharyngeal bone

---

36 Dace, *Leuciscus leuciscus*.
Also illustrated: Water spider, *Argyroneta aquatica*.

COBITIDAE

The Cobitidae or loaches are small, elongate bottom living fishes. They have no teeth, one dorsal fin and are characterised by having numerous barbels around the mouth. They are largely nocturnal in their habits and although there are numerous species to be found in Asia, only two are indigenous to Britain. Some of the Asian species have been imported as aquarium fish but none appear to have escaped to form feral populations.

37 Stone loach

Noemacheilus barbatulus, Linnaeus 1758

Distribution

The indigenous Stone loach is widespread and common in Wales, Ireland and most of England except the extreme south west. It is absent from the north of Scotland.

Habitat

Although found on the margins of some stony lakes the usual haunts of the Stone loach are clear streams and rivers with beds of stones.

Spawning

In April and May the males and to some extent the females develop spawning tubercles on the pectoral fins when yellow eggs measuring just under 1mm in diameter are deposited among plants and gravel in running water. They hatch after about two weeks when the larvae are 3mm long.

Size

The length of mature adults ranges from 8 to 12cm and some specimens, usually females, grow to 16cm.

Diet

The Stone loach is largely inactive during daylight and feeds at night close to the bottom on a variety of small invertebrates, crustaceans and molluscs.

Identification and similar species

The Stone loach is an elongate fish with no scales and six barbels around the mouth. The colouration is variable but usually the back is dark brown, the sides yellowish brown mottled with darker irregular patches and the belly is creamy yellow.

Spined loach, Cobitus taenia

The Stone loach can be separated from the Spined loach by the absence of a spine beneath its eye. In addition the body of the Spined loach is minutely scaled and the barbels are shorter than those of the Stone loach.

No hybrids involving the Stone loach have been recorded from British waters.

See also plate 38.

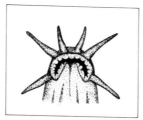

Mouth structure

---

37 Stone loach, *Noemacheilus barbatulus*.
Also illustrated: Brooklime, *Veronica beccabunga*; Hornwort, *Ceratophyllum demersum*.

38 Spined loach

Cobitis taenia, Linnaeus 1758

Distribution

Due to its secretive habits the indigenous Spined loach is thought to be a rare species. It is certainly not as widespread as the Stone loach, *Noemacheilus barbatulus* and is probably confined to the eastern Midlands of England.

Habitat

The Spined loach is usually found in small streams in which there is an abundance of plant growth amongst which it hides during daylight hours, emerging at dusk to feed. However, it also occurs in slow flowing waters where it buries itself in soft mud during the day.

Spawning

The spawning season is from April to June when yellowish eggs measuring just under 1mm in diameter are attached to plants or to stones. They hatch in about a fortnight when the larvae measure from 2 to 4mm in length.

Size

The Spined loach is usually a little smaller than the Stone loach, the average adult length being about 8cm, but there are records of fish measuring over 13cm.

Diet

This species feeds only at night, and little is known of its diet. It appears to eat a variety of bottom living plant matter and invertebrates.

Identification and similar species

The body is long with tiny, almost imperceptible scales and there are six short barbels around the mouth. The back is dark brown, the sides paler, often yellowish and the belly is pale yellow or whitish. On each side there are one or two rows of about 16 darker patches which run from head to tail and which may join to form irregular lines. The fins are pale brown spotted or barred with dark brown and a sharp double pointed spine is present below each eye. This spine is often indistinct, being covered by a fold of skin, but it is always present.

Stone loach, Noemacheilus barbatulus
The differences between the two loaches are listed under Stone loach, page 78.

No hybrids involving the Spined loach have been recorded from British waters.
See also plate 37.

Mouth structure

---

38 Spined loach, *Cobitis taenia*.
Also illustrated : Crayfish, *Astacus pallipes*.

The Gasterosteidae or sticklebacks are widespread
throughout much of Asia, Europe and North America,
and are extremely adaptable to their surroundings. Two
species are found in fresh water in Britain and both are
well known for their nest building and for the attention
they pay their eggs and also for their strict defence of their
territories.

39 Three spined stickleback

Gasterosteus aculeatus, Linnaeus 1758

Distribution

The Three spined stickleback is one of the most abundant
fishes in Britain. It is indigenous and found in every
county.

Habitat

This Stickleback is tolerant of virtually any type of water,
be it fresh, brackish or salt although it tends to be less
common in small muddy or weedy ponds where its place
is taken by the Ten spined stickleback, *Pungitius pungitius*.

Spawning

In May and June yellow eggs measuring 1.5mm in
diameter are laid in clumps in a nest which is built by the
male from plant matter on the bottom in still water. The
male tends the eggs until they hatch after one or two weeks
when the larvae measure from 3 to 5mm in length. They
grow fairly quickly and may reach a length of 5cm after
one year when maturity is reached.

Size

Mature Three spined sticklebacks may measure as little
as 2cm in length or as much as 10cm but they average
about 4 or 5cm.

Diet

The food of the Three spined stickleback consists almost
entirely of a wide variety of invertebrates.

Identification and similar species

The back is dark green or blackish, the sides are silvery
and the belly is white, although in the spawning season
the male develops a conspicuous red belly. The main
distinguishing features are the three spines on the back,
the third of which lies close to the dorsal fin and which is
usually smaller than the first two.

There is considerable variation in the arrangement of
the large bony plates on the sides of the Three spined
stickleback and this variation has caused three types of
the fish to be recognised in Britain although others are
known from the mainland of Europe, One type, the
Trachura, has a complete row of scales from head to tail;
the Semi-armata has a variable incomplete row, and the
Leiurus is scaleless.

Ten spined stickleback, Pungitius pungitius
The two Sticklebacks can easily be separated by the
number of spines on their backs.

No hybrids involving the Three spined stickleback have
been recorded from British waters.
See also plate 40.

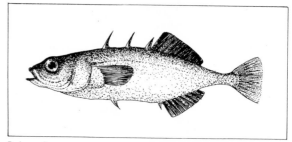

Leiurus form

---

39 Three spined stickleback, *Gasterosteus aculeatus*, male Trachura
in breeding colours (top), female Trachura (centre), and Semi
armata (bottom)
Also illustrated: Canadian pondweed, *Elodea canadensis*.

40 Ten spined stickleback

Pungitius pungitius, Linnaeus 1758

Distribution

The indigenous Ten spined stickleback is widespread throughout the British Isles and although its presence is sporadic it is locally common. It is rare in Wales, the south west of England, western Ireland and Scotland.

Habitat

In some waters this species shares its habitat with the Three spined stickleback, *Gasterosteus aculeatus* but it is more likely to be found in overgrown ditches and ponds which have a muddy bottom and which may be quite shallow (i.e. waters which are not favoured by the Three spined stickleback). It occurs in brackish water but is not so tolerant of salinity as its relative.

Spawning

Between April and July yellowish eggs measuring just over 1 mm in diameter are deposited in clumps in nests composed of plant matter built by the male in still or slow flowing water. One male may attract more than one female to lay in his nest and he guards the eggs and larvae which hatch in about ten days. About a week after hatching the young disperse to live amid the cover of weeds and do not enter open water until the autumn. Maturity is reached within a year when the fish measure between 3 or 4cm in length.

Size

The Ten spined stickleback is generally smaller than the Three spined stickleback and rarely grows to a length of more than 7cm. Adults are usually about 4cm long.

Diet

The diet is very variable and consists mainly of crustaceans, insect larvae, and small worms. Feeding is less intensive in the winter and spring.

Identification and similar species

The back and sides are usually olive green or brownish and the belly is silver. During the spawning season the colouration of the males becomes more intense and the belly often has a bluish tinge. The dorsal and anal fins are placed well back and are similar in size and shape. The pelvic fins consists of a single spine and one ray and there are between 8 and 10 spines on the back ahead of the dorsal fin.

Three spined stickleback, Gasterosteus aculeatus

The Three spined stickleback has only three spines on the back.

Fifteen spined stickleback, Spinachia spinachia

The Fifteen spined stickleback, which is an entirely marine species and not included in this book, sometimes enters estuaries and can be distinguished from the Ten spined stickleback by its more elongate body and by its 14 to 16 spines on the back.

No hybrids involving the Ten spined stickleback have been recorded from British waters.

See also plate 39.

---

40 Ten spined stickleback, *Pungitius pungitius*, non-breeding (top and bottom), and male in breeding colours (centre). Also illustrated: Silver water beetle, *Hydrous piceus*; Marsh foxtail grass, *Alopecurus geniculatus*; Horned pondweed, *Zannichellia palustris*.

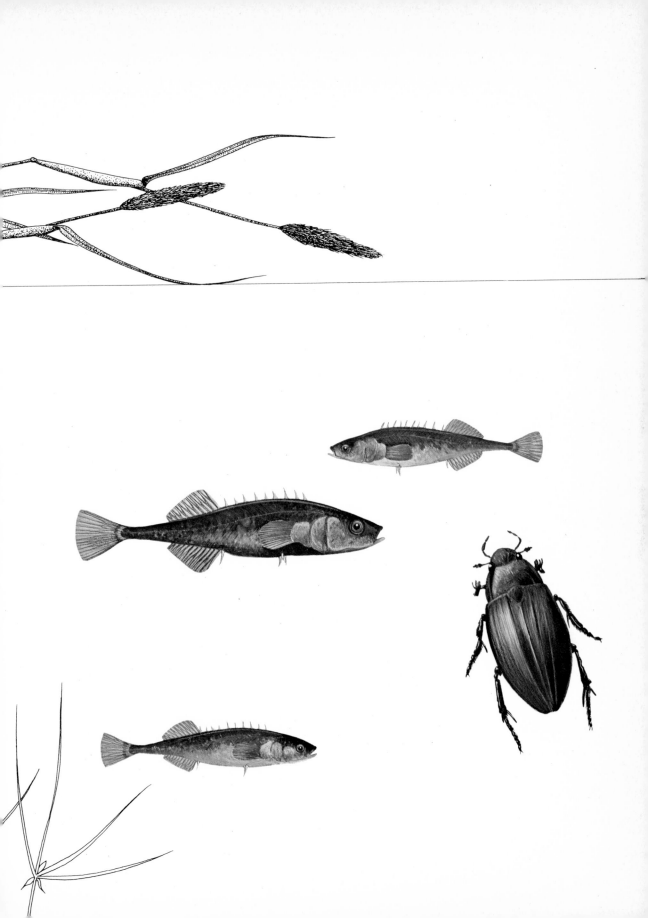

The Siluridae are scaleless catfishes with long barbels and a very long anal fin. There are several species in Asia but only two in Europe, one of which has been introduced to British waters.

41 Wels

Siluris glanis, Linnaeus 1758

Distribution

The Wels has been introduced to a few waters in England, the most dense populations occurring in lakes in the south Midlands, particularly in Bedfordshire.

Habitat

Although found in large rivers and to some extent in brackish water in the mainland of Europe, the Wels is primarily a fish of rich weedy lakes, preferably those with a muddy bottom. It is largely nocturnal and remains hidden during the day.

Spawning

In May and June large yellow eggs measuring 3mm in diameter are attached to weeds in still water and are guarded by the male until they hatch when the larvae are 7mm in length. They grow quickly, the average length after one year being about 20cm.

Size

The Wels is potentially one of the biggest fishes found in fresh water in Britain, the average adult length varying between 50 and 100cm. However, it can grow much bigger than this and lengths of around 500cm have been recorded from the mainland of Europe.

Diet

Young Wels feed mainly on invertebrates and turn gradually to a diet consisting almost entirely of fish after about a year. This diet is supplemented by amphibians, the young of water fowl, small mammals and other creatures.

Identification and similar species

The Wels has a blackish green back and a creamy white belly while the sides are blotched and generally intermediate in colour between the back and the belly. The head is broad and flat with a wide mouth and six barbels, two on the upper jaw and four on the lower. All the fins are relatively small except the anal fin which is about half the length of the fish.

No hybrids involving the Wels have been recorded from British waters.

Another catfish, the Brown bullhead, *Ictalurus nebulosus* (family Ictaluridae) is quite commonly kept in ornamental ponds and aquaria. Although not yet recorded as a wild species in Britain feral populations may exist in one or two waters. It can be separated from the Wels by its smaller size (rarely more than 35cm long), its much shorter anal fin and its eight barbels.

Brown bullhead, *Ictalurus nebulosus*.

---

41 Wels, *Siluris glanis*.
Also illustrated: Tufted duck, *Aythya fuligula*.

The Anguilladae or eels occur in Europe, Africa, Asia and in North and South America. The sixteen species are all elongate fishes with no pelvic fins and all are cata-dromous. Only one species is found in British waters.

42 Eel

Anguilla anguilla, Linnaeus 1758

Distribution

The Eel, an indigenous species, is common throughout the whole of the British Isles.

Habitat

Almost any type of water is suitable for the Eel whether still, flowing, fresh or salt, and its ability to travel over land, usually at night in wet conditions, accounts for its presence in closed ponds.

Spawning

Spawning takes place in the Sargasso Sea in the western Atlantic and the clear eggs which measure 1 mm in diameter have never been found elsewhere. The larvae take between two and three years to cross the Atlantic and when they enter British rivers measure about 6cm long. Their stay in fresh water lasts from eight to twenty years, the females remaining much longer than the males and at maturity they make their way back across the Atlantic to spawn, after which they die.

Size

Mature male Eels are usually only about 40cm long but females are rarely less than 50cm and often between 80 and 100cm.

Diet

In fresh water the Eel lives almost entirely on inverte-brates, especially insect larvae although larger specimens do take small fish, usually those which live on the bottom.

Identification and similar species

During most of its time in fresh water the Eel has a dark greyish brown back, yellowish sides with a white belly and relatively small eyes. On maturity however, the eyes become very much larger, the colour of the back darkens and the sides and belly become silver. The scales are minute and barely perceptible.

Lampreys, Petromyzonidae
The Eel can at once be distinguished from all three British lampreys by the structure of the mouth and by the fact that the lampreys have no paired fins.
Conger, Conger conger
In salt water the Eel could be confused with small speci-mens of the very much bigger Conger, an entirely marine species which is not included here. The two fishes can be separated by the fact that the top jaw of the Conger is longer than its lower jaw whereas at all stages of the Eel's development its lower jaw is appreciably longer.

No hybrids involving the Eel have been recorded from British waters.
See also plates 1, 2 and 3.

42 Eel, *Anguilla anguilla*, non-breeding (top), and in breeding colours (bottom).
Also illustrated: Fish leech, *Piscicola geometra*; Holly leaved naiad, *Najas marina*.

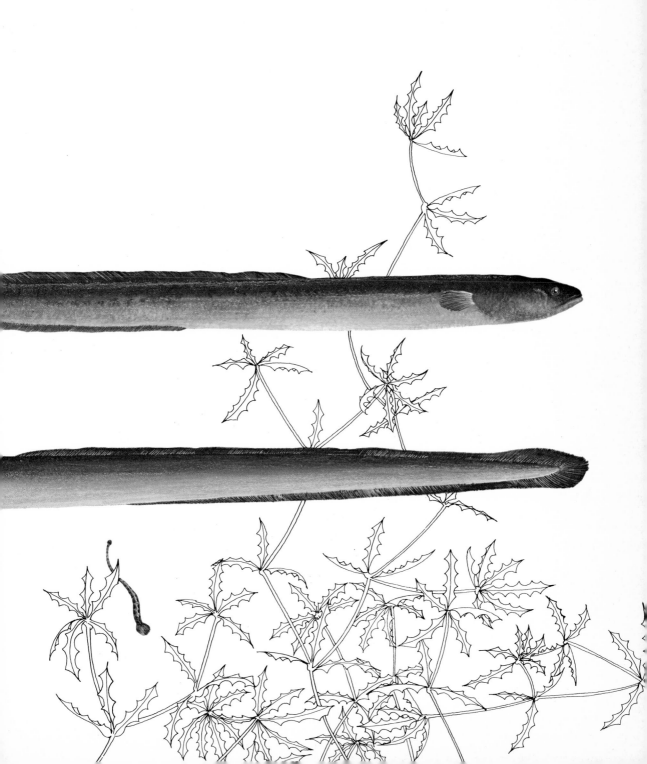

The Gadidae contain a large number of marine species which are of considerable economic importance, notably the Cod, *Gadus morhua*. They all have more than one dorsal fin and many have three, none of which contain any spines. Only one species is found in fresh water in Britain.

43 Burbot

Lota lota, Linnaeus 1758

Distribution

The Burbot has probably always been a scarce fish in England but it is now certainly rarer than it once was and is still decreasing, probably occurring only in a few rivers in East Anglia and perhaps in Yorkshire. It is absent from Wales, Scotland and Ireland.

Habitat
The Burbot is found in lakes and the lower reaches of rivers and being largely nocturnal spends most of the day in holes in banks, under boulders or concealed in some similar way.

Spawning
The Burbot tends to form small spawning shoals between December and March, when large numbers of pale yellow or transparent eggs measuring just over 1mm in diameter are laid on the river bed in fairly shallow water. They hatch between four and six weeks later when the larvae measure 3mm in length. After a year they are about 16cm long and they mature when from two to three years old.

Size
The length of adult Burbot varies between 30 and 50cm although specimens of 80 to 90cm have been recorded.

Diet
Young Burbot feed on invertebrates of many types but mature specimens are primarily fish eaters.

Identification
The back and sides are usually greenish brown with darker mottling and the belly, especially that part forward of the anal fin, is paler and may be white. Burbot in their first year of life are more boldly marked. There are two dorsal fins, the first is short but the second is very long containing on average 75 rays, and the anal fin is also long. There is one very small barbel by each nostril, and a single long one on the lower jaw. The scales are minute, often being almost invisible as they are deeply embedded in the skin.

There are no similar species and no hybrids involving the Burbot have been recorded from British waters.

43 Burbot, *Lota lota*.
Also illustrated: Horse chestnut, *Aesculus hippocastanum*.

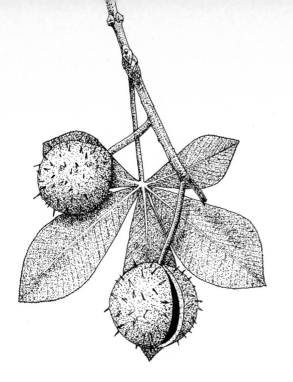

The Serranidae are found throughout the world, mainly in salt water. Two species occur in the sea around Britain but only the Sea bass occurs in fresh water.

44 Sea bass

Dicentrarchus labrax, Linnaeus 1758

Distribution

The indigenous Sea bass lives in all coastal habitats and although it seems to prefer rocky coasts it is often found in brackish water and sometimes swims well up rivers into fresh water.

Spawning

Spawning takes place at sea between June and August when colourless eggs measuring a little over 1mm in diameter are shed. They are usually attached to rocks or plants although they are occasionally left to drift in open water.

Size

Sea bass mature when about 30cm long and may grow up to 70 or 80cm.

Diet

The diet consists of crustaceans, invertebrates and a variety of fish especially small shoaling species.

Identification

The Sea bass has a greyish blue back with blue or silvery sides, a yellowish or white belly and two dorsal fins, the first of which is spiny. The head is partially scaled and there is usually a dark irregular patch on the operculum. Rarely there may be dark spots on the back of adult fish although young specimens up to 10 or 12cm in length almost always have black spots on the back and sides. The scales are fairly large, there being 66 to 75 along the lateral line.

There are no similar species and no hybrids involving the Sea bass have been recorded from British waters.

44 Sea bass, *Dicentrarchus labrax.*

The Centrarchidae or sunfish family contains many North American species which superficially resemble the Percidae. Three of these have been introduced to the British Isles and all are rare, although in their natural habitat they breed profusely and once well established may spread quickly.

45 Large mouth bass

Micropterus salmoides, Lacépède 1802

Distribution

The Large mouth bass was introduced from North America to Europe late in the nineteenth century and later to England, where it is very local and rare. The best established colony is in a disused clay pit near Wareham in Dorset. Other colonies in Surrey are not so well established and are probably in decline.

Habitat

The Large mouth bass is best suited to lakes which are rich in plant growth but it can also survive in the lower reaches of rivers.

Spawning

Between March and May the female excavates a shallow depression in still water which is often lined with plant debris. Sticky yellow eggs which measure 2mm in diameter are deposited in clumps in the nest and these and the larvae are protected by the male. They mature in two or three years when they measure from 20 to 25cm in length.

Size

Mature Large mouth bass usually measure from 20 to 35cm but some specimens reach 45cm, while in North America they grow to 60 or even 70cm.

Diet

Young Large mouth bass eat a variety of invertebrates while larger specimens also take fish.

Identification and similar species

The Large mouth bass has a dark brownish green back, the sides are green, the belly is pale green or whitish and there is usually a black irregular line between the operculum and the caudal fin but this is often indistinct. There are two dorsal fins which just touch where the spiny first meets the soft rayed second, and both the head and mouth are large. There are 65 to 70 scales along the lateral line.

Pumpkinseed, Lepomis gibbosus and Rock bass, Amblopites rupestris
Both these closely related species are deeper in the body than the Large mouth bass, and both have a single dorsal fin which is clearly divided into a spiny first part and a soft rayed second part. In addition both species have less than 50 scales along the lateral line.

No hybrids involving the Large mouth bass have been recorded from British waters.
See also plates 46 and 47.

45 Large mouth bass, *Micropterus salmoides*.
Also illustrated: Great bladderwort, *Utricularia vulgaris*.

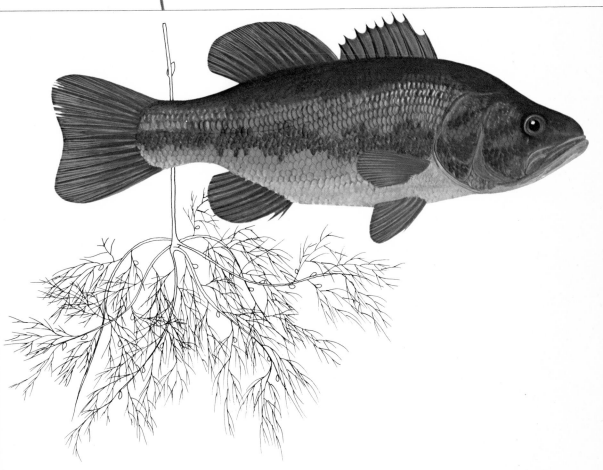

46 Pumpkinseed

Lepomis gibbosus, Linnaeus 1758

Distribution

The Pumpkinseed was introduced from America to the mainland of Europe at about the turn of the century and later to England where it is now a very rare species, occurring only in lakes in Somerset and perhaps in one or two localities in Suffolk.

Habitat

The Pumpkinseed inhabits lakes which are rich in vegetation and to a lesser extent it is found in the lower reaches of rivers.

Spawning

Between May and August the Pumpkinseed lays yellowish eggs measuring 2mm in diameter which are deposited in clumps usually in a hollow on the sandy bed of still or slow flowing water. The eggs and larvae are usually guarded by the male until they disperse.

Size

Although in America the Pumpkinseed sometimes attains a length of 25cm, in England the average is between 10 and 15cm.

Diet

The Pumpkinseed eats a variety of invertebrates and small fish.

Identification and similar species

The Pumpkinseed is a deep bodied fish and although the colour is variable it usually has a dark greenish blue back, paler greenish blue sides with orange spots and a whitish green belly. The sides are often more or less striped vertically while the operculum usually has some horizontal stripes and a red spot at its tip. There are 38 to 49 scales along the lateral line.

Rock bass, Amblopites rupestris
The Rock bass does not have a red spot at the tip of the operculum and it always has more than four spines in the anal fin; the Pumpkinseed always has less than four spines in the anal fin.

Large mouth bass, Micropterus salmoides
The Large mouth bass is a more elongate species than the Pumpkinseed and has more than 50 scales along the lateral line; the Pumpkinseed always has less than 50. In addition the Large mouth bass has two dorsal fins which just touch where they meet.

No hybrids involving the Pumpkinseed have been recorded from British waters.

See also plates 45 and 47.

46 Pumpkinseed, *Lepomis gibbosus*.
Also illustrated: Tadpole of Common frog, *Rana temporaria*; Shining pondweed, *Potamogeton lucens*.

47 Rock bass

Ambloplites rupestris, Rafinesque-Schmaltz 1817

Distribution

The Rock bass, a native of North America and Canada, has been introduced to England but it is very rare, being found mainly in lakes in Oxfordshire.

Habitat

Like the other members of the Centrarchidae found in British waters the Rock bass favours lakes which are rich in plant growth but it may also occur in the lower reaches of rivers.

Spawning

The breeding season of the Rock bass lasts from May to August when yellow eggs which measure 2mm in diameter are deposited in clumps in nests on the sandy bottom of slow flowing or still water.

Size

The length of adults varies between 12 and 20cm although some specimens reach a length of 30cm.

Diet

Like the rest of the Centrarchidae the Rock bass is primarily a fish eater although a variety of insects, crustaceans and molluscs are taken, especially by smaller specimens.

Identification and similar species

The Rock bass is a deep bodied fish with a large mouth and a single dorsal fin which is clearly divided into two parts, the first part of which is spined while the second part is composed of soft rays. There are also short spines on the front part of the anal fin. The back is dark greenish brown, the sides paler greenish brown and the belly greenish white. Each scale, of which there are 36 to 44 along the lateral line, has a darker centre which has the effect of giving the Rock bass a striped appearance and there is a distinct black spot on the operculum.

Pumpkinseed, Lepomis gibbosus

The Pumpkinseed is a more colourful species than the Rock bass and has a red spot on the operculum. It has less than four spines in the anal fin, whereas the anal fin of the Rock bass has more than four spines.

Large mouth bass, Micropterus salmoides

This is a more elongate species than the Rock bass and it has two dorsal fins which just touch. It has more than 50 scales along the lateral line.

No hybrids involving the Rock bass have been recorded from British waters.

See also plates 45 and 46.

---

47 Rock bass, *Ambloplites rupestris*.
Also illustrated: Small bur reed, *Sparganium minimum*.

Most of the Percidae have two dorsal fins, the first of which is spined and the second of which contains mainly soft rays. There are also spines on the anal fin and on the pelvic fins which are situated well forward, being beneath the pectoral fins. All three British members of the Percidae inhabit lakes and the lower reaches of rivers and all three are carnivorous.

48 Perch

Perca fluviatilis, Linnaeus 1758

Distribution

The Perch is indigenous to Britain and is widespread and common although it is scarce in high altitudes, being most frequently found in the lowlands of the south of England, the Midlands, and East Anglia.

Habitat
The Perch is a sedentary species which prefers canals and slow flowing rivers and lakes where it often forms large shoals. It is also found to a lesser extent in quite fast flowing rivers.

Spawning
Between April and June white eggs measuring from 2 to 2.5mm in diameter are laid amongst dense vegetation in shallow water. The eggs are contained in long mucous covered threads which are entwined among the plants. They hatch in two to three weeks when the larvae are about 8mm long, and they mature two to four years later when 15 to 25cm long.

Size
The normal adult length is 20 to 30cm although Perch can grow to 40cm or more

Diet
Young Perch live on invertebrates while bigger specimens also take fish.

Identification and similar species
The Perch can usually be distinguished by the dark bars on the sides and the black spot at the rear of the first dorsal fin, although the dark bars are not always distinct. The body colour is dark brownish green on the back, yellowish green on the sides and more or less white on the belly. Occasionally specimens are found where the body colour is much more red than that illustrated and even bluish forms are not unknown. The pelvic, anal and caudal fins are reddish and there are 62 to 74 scales along the lateral line.

Ruffe, Gymocephalus cernua
Small Perch can be confused with Ruffe but the Perch has two distinct dorsal fins whereas the Ruffe has a single fin which is clearly divided into two parts.

Zander, Stizostedion lucioperca
Both Zander and Perch have vertical dark bands running down the sides of the body although they are not so well defined in the Zander which is a more slender fish and is without a black spot at the rear of the first dorsal fin. The bases of each dorsal fin of the Zander are more or less equal in length. In the Perch the first is longer.

No hybrids involving the Perch have been recorded from British waters.
See also plates 49 and 50.

48 Perch, *Perca fluviatilis*.
Also illustrated: Silver water beetle, *Hydrous piceus*; Reed, *Phragmites communis*.

49 Ruffe

Gymnocephalus cernua, Linnaeus 1758

Distribution

The Ruffe is indigenous to Britain and is found throughout England south of Yorkshire but the population is
most dense in the Midlands, especially towards the east.
It is absent from Scotland and Ireland.

Habitat

A bottom living species, the Ruffe frequents canals and
the lower reaches of rivers and is also found in lakes. There
is a tendency for the fish to move to smaller streams in
summer after spawning.

Spawning

Spawning shoals are formed from March to May and the
pale yellow eggs, which are contained in long sticky
strands and which measure just under 1mm in diameter
are laid in shallow slow flowing water among plants.
They hatch in eight to ten days when the larvae are 3 to
4mm long and they mature between one and two years
later at about 8cm in length.

Size

The adult length is usually between 12 and 18cm at five
to six years although in good conditions they can grow to
22cm.

Diet

The Ruffe feeds on the larvae of aquatic animals, mainly
insects and small molluscs and also on fish eggs and fry.

Identification and similar species

Superficially resembling the Perch, *Perca fluviatilis*, the
Ruffe has a greenish brown back with pale brown or
yellowish sides and a whitish yellow belly. The back and
sides are covered irregularly with darker spots or patches.
There are no scales on the head and 35 to 40 scales along
the lateral line. The dorsal and caudal fins have rows of
dark spots on the membranes and the pectoral fins are
often pinkish.

Perch, Perca fluviatilis

The Perch is the fish most likely to be confused with the
Ruffe but it has two distinct dorsal fins.

No hybrids involving the Ruffe have been recorded from
British waters. See also plate 48.

49 Ruffe, *Gymnocephalus cernua*.
Also illustrated: Water boatman, *Notonecta glauca*; Horned
pondweed, *Zannichellia palustris*.

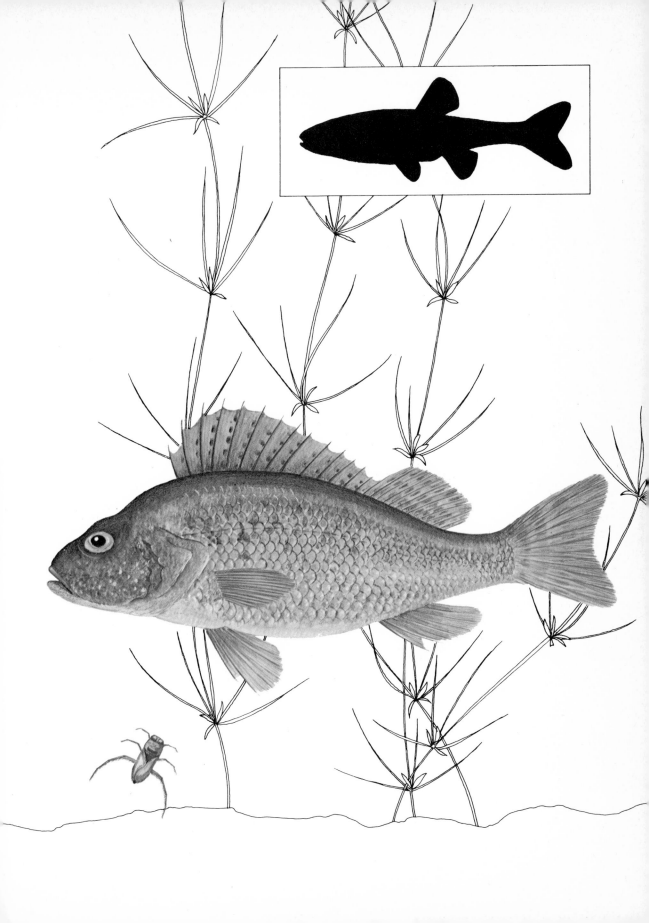

50 Zander

Stizostedion lucioperca, Linnaeus 1758

Distribution

The Zander was introduced to British waters on various occasions between the late nineteenth and mid twentieth centuries and although local it is common in some waters, notably in some Bedfordshire lakes and in the Ouse and other rivers in Cambridgeshire. It appears to be extending its range, and in 1976 an apparently artificially introduced colony was discovered in a Nottinghamshire lake which has direct access to the Severn river system.

Habitat

Although the waters in which the Zander naturally occurs are wide, shallow rivers and lakes, it has been introduced to many other habitat types where it thrives. In England it is found chiefly in lakes which are rich in vegetation, and slow flowing rivers.

Spawning

The Zander spawns between April and June in still, shallow water when clumps of yellowish eggs measuring 1.25mm in diameter are deposited amongst plants. Both parents remain near the eggs until they hatch after about a week when the larvae measure from 5 to 6mm in length. They grow quickly and mature when from 30 to 40cm long and between two and four years old.

Size

The Zander grows to an average length of between 30 and 60cm and in favourable conditions can reach a length of over 100cm.

Diet

This species is entirely carnivorous and eats a wide variety of invertebrates and fish.

Identification and similar species

The Zander has an elongate body with large jaws and two dorsal fins, the first of which is spiny. The back is greyish green, the sides pale green usually marked with from eight to ten vertical bars and the belly is white. The dorsal and caudal fins are pale greyish brown and flecked with rows of small spots but there is no large dark patch on the rear of the first dorsal fin. The pectoral and pelvic fins are whitish and unspotted, the head is sparsely scaled and there are 80 to 95 scales along the lateral line.

Perch, Perca fluviatilis

The Perch is a much less elongate fish than the Zander and can be distinguished by its dark spot on the rear of the first dorsal fin and by its reddish pelvic, anal and caudal fins.

No hybrids involving the Zander have been recorded from British waters.

See also plate 48.

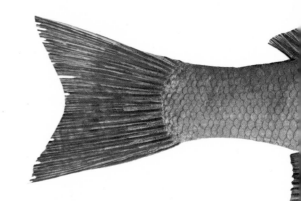

It has been suggested that a closely related species may have been introduced to some waters in Cambridgeshire during the first half of this century. However, the presence of this fish, the Walleye, *S. vitreum*, from North America has never been recorded with certainty. It is very similar in appearance to the Zander but like the Perch it has a distinct black spot on the rear of the first dorsal fin. In addition its head is almost entirely scaled, the pectoral and pelvic fins are marked with dark patches and the whole fish has a generally more spotted appearance than the Zander. Any 'Zander' with these characteristics should be referred to a competent authority for identification.

50 Zander, *Stizostedion lucioperca.*
Also illustrated: Common frog, *Rana temporaria*; Broad leaved pondweed, *Potamogeton natans.*

The Gobiidae or gobies are small fish, most of which live on the sea bed in shallow water and of the fifteen known European species only one is found in fresh water in the British Isles.

51 Common goby

Pomatoschistus microps, Krøyer 1840

Distribution

The Common goby is found around the entire coastline of the British Isles. It is indigenous and often abundant, although less common in Scotland.

Habitat

Typically a fish of rock pools in intertidal areas, the Common goby is also found to some extent in estuaries brackish water and also in fresh water, but it is never found far from the sea.

Spawning

The pear-shaped colourless eggs which are about 1mm long are attached to stones, and especially to empty bivalve shells in the sea or brackish water, between May and July. They are guarded by the male until they hatch when the larvae measure 3 or 4mm in length and they mature in one year at a length of 3 or 4cm.

Size

The usual adult length is from 4 to 6cm but sometimes specimens are found which measure 7 or even 8cm.

Diet

The Common goby feeds on a variety of small crustaceans particularly small shrimps.

Identification and similar species

As a family the Gobiidae present a baffling array of similar species although the only member found in fresh water in Britain is the Common goby. Its colour is variable, ranging from grey to brown on the back and sides with rows of small dark spots which may form irregular lines and the belly is paler. There are two dorsal fins, the first of which is spiny, there is almost always a dark patch on the upper forward edge of the pectoral fin and there are 43 to 50 scales along the lateral line. The most striking feature of this and indeed of most other gobies is the fusion of the pelvic fins by a membrane to form a weak sucking organ which is capable of holding the fish secure to a solid object, so long as the current is not too strong.

In the spawning season the males have dark vertical bars along the sides, a reddish belly and are more intensely coloured.

Bullhead, Cottus gobio

The pelvic fins of the Bullhead are separate and its head is considerably larger than that of the Common goby.

No hybrids involving the Common goby have been recorded from British waters.

See also plate 52.

51 Common goby, *Potamoschistus microps*, male in breeding colours (top), and female (bottom).
Also illustrated: Horned pondweed, *Zannichellia palustris*.

COTTIDAE

The Cottidae or bullheads are a large family of mainly small bottom living fish. Over three hundred species are known throughout the world but only one is found in fresh water in Britain.

52 Bullhead

Cottus gobio, Linnaeus 1758

Distribution

The Bullhead is indigenous but is more or less confined to England and Wales where it is common. It is absent from Ireland and scarce in Scotland.

Habitat
The Bullhead lives on the bottom of fast flowing stony streams and rivers and to some extent on the margins of stony lakes. It is a sedentary fish and is largely nocturnal, spending the daylight hours concealed beneath stones and other cover.

Spawning
Between February and May the female lays yellow eggs measuring 2.5mm in diameter, which are unusually large for her size. Consequently relatively few are laid and these are deposited in a clump hidden in a crevice which is guarded by the male until the eggs hatch in two to four weeks. The 6mm long larvae live off their yolk sacs for up to two weeks after which they gradually disperse. They mature in two years when about 8cm long.

Size
The Bullhead is a small fish and rarely exceeds 16cm in length. The normal adult length is between 9 and 14cm.

Diet
Invertebrates form the major part of the diet of the Bullhead but larger specimens also eat the eggs and fry of other fish.

Identification and similar species
The Bullhead has a large head and mouth with a single spine on the pre-operculum and the body is devoid of scales. It is dark brown or almost black on the back, the sides are mottled brown or yellowish, the fins are large and all but the pelvic fins are marked with irregular yellowish lines. The male has a larger mouth than the female and tends to be darker in colour.
Common goby, Pomatoschistus microps
The pelvic fins of the Common goby are fused together to form a weak sucking organ whereas those of the Bullhead are separate.

No hybrids involving the Bullhead have been recorded from British waters.
See also plate 51.

---

52 Bullhead, *Cottus gobio*.
Also illustrated: Banded agrion damselfly, *Agrion splendens*.

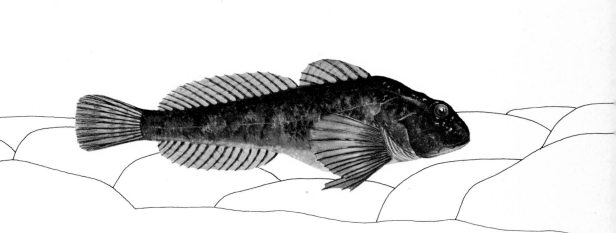

The Mugilidae are marine shoaling fishes which are found particularly during the summer in estuaries, harbours and brackish water. Three closely related species are commonly found in British waters and these are often all given the name Grey mullet. They all have two dorsal fins, the first of which contains four spines and all have large scales which extend on to the head. None of the mullets has a lateral line.

53 Thick lipped mullet

Crenimugil labrosus, Risso 1826
Distribution

The indigenous Thick lipped mullet is the most common of the mullets, being found around the entire coastline of the British Isles although it is less common in the north.

Habitat
The Thick lipped mullet inhabits inshore waters, the lower reaches of rivers and estuaries, where it is most numerous in spring and summer when it often swims in shoals very near the surface.

Spawning
Most spawning probably takes place to the south of Britain, although to some extent it does occur in British waters when clear eggs measuring 1mm in diameter are shed in open water in April and May. They drift with the tide and hatch in about a week when the larvae are 3mm long. They mature between two and four years later.

Size
This is the largest of the mullets and while the average adult length is about 45 to 55cm some specimens attain lengths of over 80cm.

Diet
The food of the Thick lipped mullet is a diverse combination of small invertebrates and plants, especially algae.

Identification and similar species
The back is dark greenish or bluish grey, the sides are silvery grey with from six to eight longitudinal darker lines and the belly is white. The upper lip is very thick with two rows of small warts. All the fins are greyish but the lower fins are sometimes white and there are 44 to 47 lateral scales.

For the differences between this and the other mullets see under Golden mullet, *Chelon auratus*, on page 112.

53 Thin lipped mullet

Chelon ramada, Risso 1826

Distribution

The indigenous Thin lipped mullet is found around most of the coastline of Britain although it is rare off Scotland and Northern Ireland and is uncommon along the North Sea coast.

Habitat
Although this species is not so common as the Thick lipped mullet, *Crenimugil labrosus*, it is more likely to be met with in rivers as it tends to be more tolerant of water where the salinity is low.

Spawning
See under Thick lipped mullet.

Size
The average adult length is between 30 and 40cm, while the maximum is 50cm.

Diet
See under Thick lipped mullet.

Identification and similar species
The Thin lipped mullet has a greyish blue back, silvery sides with from six to eight longitudinal darker lines and a white belly. The fins are greyish and may sometimes have a yellowish tinge. There are 44 to 47 lateral scales and the body shape and arrangement of fins are virtually identical to the Thick lipped mullet. The differences between this species and the other mullets are given under Golden mullet, *Chelon auratus*, on page 112.

No hybrids involving either the Thick lipped mullet or the Thin lipped mullet have been recorded from British waters.

53 Thin lipped mullet, *Chelon ramada* (top), and Thick lipped mullet, *Crenimugil labrosus* (bottom).

54 Golden mullet

Chelon auratus, Risso 1810

Distribution

The Golden mullet is an indigenous species which occurs locally in estuaries and coastal waters. It may be found along almost any stretch of the coastline of the British Isles but seems to be less common in the south east of England, in the Irish Sea and Scotland.

Habitat

The Golden mullet is found in shoals in estuaries and brackish water as well as in harbours and docks and in fresh water it is most likely to be seen in summer.

Spawning

Spawning takes place during April and May when clear eggs measuring 1mm in diameter are left to float with the tide in inshore waters. On hatching the larvae measure only 2 to 3mm in length but they grow fairly quickly reaching 8 to 12cm after a year.

Size

The Golden mullet rarely reaches a length of more than 45cm and the normal adult length is from 30 to 35cm.

Diet

Relatively little is known about the biology of the Golden mullet and its diet probably consists mainly of various seaweeds together with some invertebrates.

Identification and similar species

The Golden mullet has a bluish grey back, greyish or silvery sides usually with from six to eight longitudinal darker lines, a golden or yellowish tinge and a pale grey or white belly. Conspicuous golden patches are present on the operculum and the body shape and arrangement of fins are similar to those of the Thick lipped mullet, *Crenimugil labrosus*, although the colouration of the fins often tends to be yellowish. There are 40 to 46 lateral scales.

Thick lipped mullet, Crenimugil labrosus and *Thin lipped mullet, Chelon ramada.*

All three mullets are superficially very similar. The Thick lipped can be distinguished from the Thin lipped and Golden mullets by its swollen upper lip. The Golden and Thin lipped mullets can be confused especially as the colouration of the Golden mullet does not always live up to its name. However, these two can usually be identified regardless of colour by bearing the following points in mind. The bone between the corner of the mouth and the eye of the Thin lipped mullet is rounded and it has small teeth on the upper lip. The Golden mullet has a more or less pointed bone between the corner of the mouth and the eye and it has moderately well spaced teeth on the upper lip.

No hybrids involving the Golden mullet have been recorded from British waters.
See also plate 53.

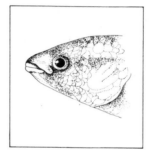 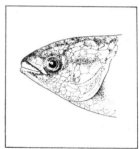

Head of the Thin lipped mullet, *Chelon ramada*

Head of the Golden mullet, *Chelon auratus*

A closely related species, the Grey mullet, *Mugil labeo* from southern Europe, is sometimes found along the south coast of England. It is smaller than the other mullets, averaging about 18cm in length. The upper lip is very thick but it can be separated from the Thick lipped mullet because the lip is smooth, not warty. In other respects it resembles the other mullets.

Head of the Grey mullet, *Mugil labeo*

54 Golden mullet, *Chelon auratus*.

Almost all the Pleuronecetidae are marine flatfishes many of which form a valuable food source. Eight species are found in European waters, but only one of these occurs regularly in fresh water in Britain.

55 Flounder

Platichthys flesus, Linnaeus 1758

Distribution

Of all the marine species found in fresh water in the British Isles, the Flounder is by far the most frequent, being found not only in estuaries and rivers but also in lakes which are easily accessible from the sea. Generally regarded as ubiquitous it seems to be most common along the east coast of England.

Habitat

The Flounder is a bottom living estuarine species which is found in the sea to depths of about fifty metres and also in rivers and lakes especially those with sandy bottoms.

Spawning

The Flounder always spawns in the sea where small eggs measuring about 0.75mm in diameter are shed in open water. They hatch in about a week when the larvae which measure 3mm in length possess the symmetrical characteristics of non-flat fish. By the time the young fish reach a length of about 25mm they have assumed the flat shape and thereafter live entirely on the bottom. They mature when between 10 and 15cm in length and from one to three years old.

Size

The average adult length is 25 to 35cm and although specimens over 40cm are uncommon they do grow to 50cm.

Diet

The Flounder is almost wholly carnivorous and feeds mainly during the summer months on a variety of crustaceans and molluscs.

Identification and similar species

The body and fins of the Flounder are dark brownish or greyish green on the eyed side with rough scales either side of the lateral line especially around the pectoral fin and also along the bases of the anal and dorsal fins. The blind side is entirely white and sometimes there is a random array of a few pale orange spots on the eyed side. The eyes are usually on the right side of the body, i.e. as shown on plate 55, but reversed specimens are not uncommon.

Plaice, Pleuronectes platessa

The plaice is an almost wholly marine species and is only rarely found in intertidal areas and is not included here. It can be distinguished from the Flounder by its large number of brilliant orange spots on the eyed side and by the fact that it has a row of at least four bony knobs between the eyes and the lateral line, whereas the Flounder does not have more than two. In addition the Plaice does not have any rough scales along the lateral line or along the bases of the fins.

Hybrids

The Flounder hybridises with the Plaice but this hybrid has only been recorded in the sea and does not appear to occur in fresh or even brackish water.

55 Flounder, *Platichthys flesus*.
Also illustrated: Shell of Common piddock, *Pholus dactylus*.

A large number of hybrids have been recorded from the mainland of Europe, but relatively few occur naturally in British waters, all of which are included here. Those European hybrids not found in Britain are: Sturgeon × Sterlet, *Acipenser sturio × A. ruthenus* (the Sterlet is the smallest of the European Acipenseridae and is confined to eastern Europe); Allis shad × Twaite shad, *Alosa alosa × A. fallax*; Salmon × Trout, *Salmo salar × S. trutta*; Rainbow trout × Brook char, *Salmo gairdneri × Salvelinus fontinalis*; Char × Brook char, *Salvelinus alpinus × S. fontinalis*; Rudd × Silver bream, *Scardinius erythrophthalmus × Blicca bjoerkna*; Roach × Silver bream, *Rutilus rutilus × B. bjoerkna*; Bream × Silver bream, *Abramis brama × B. bjoerkna*; Bleak × Silver bream, *Alburnus alburnus × B. bjoerkna* and Bleak × Rudd, *A. alburnus × S. erythrophthalmus*. Any of these hybrids except the first may well occur from time to time in British waters but so far none has been discovered.

All the hybrids are notoriously difficult to identify with certainty: even examination of pharyngeal bones of Cyprinid hybrids is not a foolproof guide to parentage as these are apt to vary, and the external features are unreliable as one hybrid will not necessarily exhibit the same percentage of parental features as another of the same type. For this reason the descriptions of external characteristics are kept to a minimum here and fish whose parentage is in doubt can usually be identified with certainty only by a competent authority. In most doubtful cases it is probably better to remain in the dark than to resort to killing the fish to examine it in detail. Also, it is important to bear in mind that a fish suspected of being a hybrid may well be a malformed or sickly true breed.

In this section the paragraphs dealing with distribution, habitat and diet are omitted as this information can be taken from those paragraphs relating to the parents. Distribution maps however, are included although these show potential distribution rather than actual records. As most hybrids are sterile, details concerning spawning are omitted and it can be generally assumed that in the wild the size of each of the hybrids is usually smaller than the larger of the parents.

56 Brown trout × Brook char

Salmo trutta × Salvelinus fontinalis

Distribution

Because the Brook char is uncommon in Britain, the hybrid between it and the Brown trout is bound to occur only very rarely. The developing eggs have a very high mortality rate and those which hatch often give rise to malformed fish. Healthy specimens are sterile and generally intermediate between the parents but are unusual in that the colouration is unlike that of either of the parents. The body colour is variable and is usually distinctively marked with darker irregular vertical bars. There are 120 to 240 scales along the lateral line.

See also plates 9 and 11.

56 Carp × Crucian carp

Cyprinus carpio × Carassius carassius

Distribution

The Carp × Crucian carp hybrid usually looks more like the Crucian carp than the Carp but it tends to grow more quickly than the Crucian carp. Barbels are not always present but normally there are two and they are smaller than those of the Carp. This is a relatively common hybrid and the fertility rate is high although most specimens found are likely to be males, the females being very rare. There are 32 to 40 scales along the lateral line.

See also plates 19 and 22.

---

56 Brown trout × Brook char, *Salmo trutta × Salvelinus fontinalis* (top), and Carp × Crucian carp, *Cyprinus carpio × Carassius carassius* (bottom).

57 Roach × Bream

Rutilus rutilus × *Abramis brama*

Distribution

This hybrid usually has the appearance of a deep bodied, very slimy Roach, but the body is not so deep as that of the Bream, nor is it so slimy. The anal fin is long although not so long as that of the Bream and usually contains between 16 and 21 rays, while there are 9 or 10 rays in the dorsal fin and from 40 to 55 scales along the lateral line. This is perhaps the most common hybrid occurring in Britain and its offspring are often fertile with the result that in some waters complex and confusing populations develop.

See also plates 27 and 33.

57 Chub × Bleak

Leuciscus cephalus × *Alburnus alburnus*

Distribution

This moderately common hybrid usually has from 45 to 50 scales along the lateral line, 8 or 9 rays in the dorsal fin and between 10 and 14 rays in the anal fin which may have either a concave or convex edge. It is occasionally fertile.

See also plates 29 and 34.

57 Roach × Bream, *Rutilus rutilus* × *Abramis brama* (top), and Chub × Bleak, *Leuciscus cephalus* × *Alburnus alburnus* (bottom). Also illustrated: Small bur reed, *Sparganium minimum*.

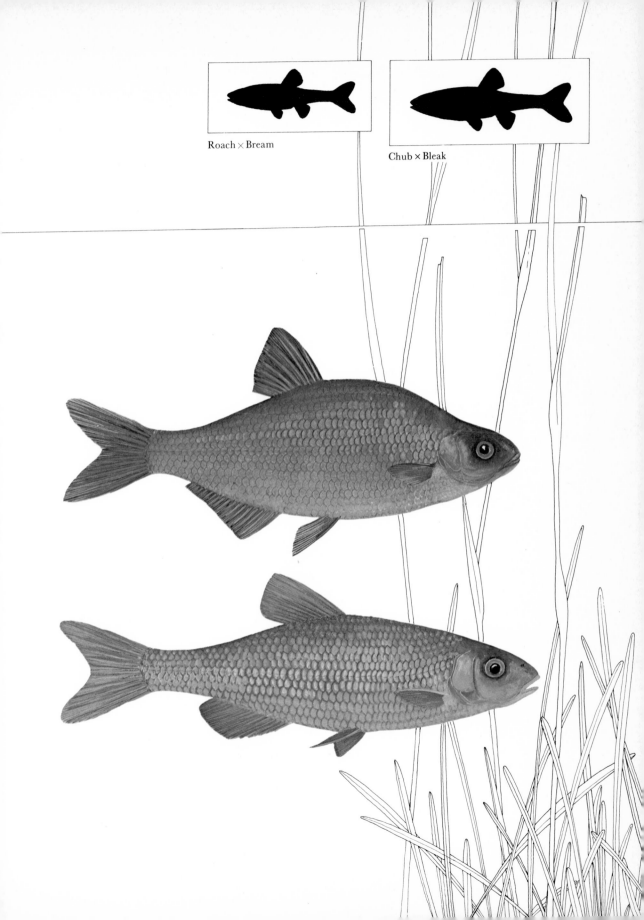

Roach × Bream

Chub × Bleak

58 Bream × Orfe

Abramis brama × Leuciscus idus

Distribution

In appearance the Bream x Orfe is rather like a deep bodied Orfe and is generally intermediate between the parents. It is usually sterile and very rare.

See also plates 27 and 35.

58 Bream × Rudd

Abramis brama × Scardinius erythrophthalmus

Distribution

The Bream × Rudd hybrid is a deep bodied fish although it is not usually so deep as the Bream. The eye is small, being not greater than one quarter of the length of the head and the front of the dorsal fin is nearer the tail than the front of the pelvic fins. The anal fin is long although not as long as that of the Bream and contains 17 to 20 rays. This hybrid is usually sterile and is scarce in most of Britain except in some Irish lakes where it is quite common.

See also plates 32 and 27.

58 Bream × Orfe, *Abramis brama × Leuciscus idus* (top), and Bream × Rudd, *A. brama × Scardinius erythrophthalmus* (bottom). Also illustrated: Canadian pondweed, *Elodea canadensis*.

59 Roach × Rudd

Rutilus rutilus × Scardinius erythrophthalmus

Distribution

The Roach × Rudd hybrid which is often fertile is some-times common in those waters where both parents occur. There are from 38 to 42 scales along the lateral line, the dorsal fin is over the rear of the base of the pelvic fins and there are usually ten rays in the anal fin. Its other physiological details are more variable than these and are unreliable as means of identification.

See also plates 32 and 33.

59 Roach × Bleak

Rutilus rutilus × Alburnus alburnus

Distribution

The Roach × Bleak hybrid is generally intermediate between the parents. There are between 45 and 52 scales along the lateral line, the dorsal fin which is placed to the rear of the base of the pelvic fins contains between 8 and 11 rays and there are 13 to 15 rays in the anal fin. This is a rare fish and is seldom fertile.

See also plates 29 and 33.

59 Roach × Rudd, *Rutilus rutilus × Scardinius erythrophthalmus* (top), and Roach × Bleak, *R. rutilus × Alburnus alburnus* (bottom). Also illustrated: Fennel leaved pondweed. *Potamogeton pectinatus.*

Roach × Rudd

Roach × Bleak

60 Dace × Bleak

Leuciscus leuciscus × Alburnus alburnus

Distribution

In appearance the Dace × Bleak is generally intermediate between the parents and usually looks like a Dace with a long anal fin and a larger than usual eye. It is usually sterile and very rare.

See also plates 29 and 36.

60 Dace × Rudd

Leuciscus leuciscus × Scardinius erythrophthalmus

Distribution

This extremely rare hybrid which is almost always sterile is generally intermediate between the parents being neither as deep in the body as the Rudd, nor as sleek as the Dace.

See also plates 32 and 36.

60 Dace × Bleak, *Leuciscus leuciscus × Alburnus alburnus* (top), and Dace × Rudd, *L. leuciscus × Scardinius erythrophthalmus* (bottom). Also illustrated: Freshwater worm, *Eiseniella tetrahedra*.

SPECIES OF DOUBTFUL STATUS

In addition to the species dealt with in the main body of
this book there are others which although of doubtful
status are noteworthy. Apart from a few which for
identification purposes are mentioned elsewhere, the
three main species are the Guppy, *Poecilia reticulata*, the
Channel catfish, *Ictalurus punctatus* and *Tilapia zillii*
which does not have an English name. In addition to
these there are always ephemeral non-breeding
populations of various catfish, angelfish, mollies and
other aquarium species which from time to time are
rejected by their owners.

Guppy, *Poecilia reticulata*

This South American guppy which is a popular aquarium
fish has bred in recent years in at least two localities in
England. One was in the River Lea in Essex where the
water was heated by the discharge of cooling water from
Hackney power station. This colony is presumably now
extinct due to the closure of the plant. The second colony
is in the St Helens canal in Lancashire where water is
heated by discharge from Pilkington glass works. So long
as this factory remains open it seems likely that this
population will remain reasonably stable. The Guppy is
a very small species rarely measuring more than 4cm long.
The colouration of the males is very variable but whatever
the ground colour, there are usually some iridescent spots
on both body and fins. The females which are larger than
the males are yellowish brown or greenish.

Channel catfish, *Ictalurus punctatus*

The Channel catfish is a native of North America and
many have been imported to Britain as aquarium stock.
For successful spawning it requires a water temperature
of about 30°C so is not likely to thrive in the wild in
Britain although it has been reported from lakes in the
London area. It has a dark brown or bluish back with
paler sides and a yellowish belly. The sides are spotted and
there are six long barbels around the mouth and two
shorter ones near the nostrils. The base of the anal fin is
more or less the same length as the body is deep and the
caudal fin is deeply forked. In its natural habitat it grows
to a length of about 60cm.

Tilapia zillii

Tilapia zillii, a native of Africa is, like the Guppy, found in
the St Helens canal adjacent to the Pilkington glass works
and is not known from any other locality. It is a relatively
deep bodied fish which grows to a length of about 25cm in
its natural habitat. The body is bluish green and is marked
with between five and seven darker vertical bars. The
dorsal fin consists of two united parts, the first part being
spiny while the soft rayed second part contains a large
black spot which is usually bordered with yellow.

INDEX

Numbers in bold type refer to plates, those in Roman type indicate the main text references and those in italic type indicate other references